T0209698

SAFE SPACES

*A Journey from a Frightened Little
Horsegirl to a Global Empowerment Leader*

MERJA K. SUMILOFF, LISA WALLACE

BALBOA.PRESS
A DIVISION OF HAY HOUSE

Balboa Press books may be ordered through booksellers or by contacting:

Balboa Press
A Division of Hay House
1663 Liberty Drive
Bloomington, IN 47403
www.balboapress.com
844-682-1282

Print information available on the last page.

ISBN: 979-8-7652-4327-5 (sc)
ISBN: 979-8-7652-4326-8 (hc)
ISBN: 979-8-7652-4325-1 (e)

Library of Congress Control Number: 2023922271

Balboa Press rev. date: 02/13/2024

DEDICATION

This book is dedicated to Peter.
You are willing to see me for <u>me</u>.

FOREWORD

Whether we accept it or not, the nature of life is progressive and cyclical. A liquid amber - Red Horse's favorite tree - blooms in the spring, thrives in the summer, loses its leaves in the autumn, and stands dormant in the winter. Every year. Without exception. Until it is ready to move on to nourish the future generations of plants.

Throughout its life, year by year, the broadleaved tree grows until it has reached its maturity to reproduce. When it begins to bear seed, it's ready to share its gifts with the community of trees around it, and if naughty ponies don't get to the saplings before they are fully rooted, a whole new generation of trees is born.

It surprises me when humans deny that we are much like those trees. We rarely exist in a vacuum; we are born, we live and contribute, and as long as we live in the hearts and minds of those we leave behind at death, we continue to nourish the generations to come.

But unlike those trees who often don't get to choose where they grow and develop, we can. You, my dear reader, and I can choose the places we occupy to grow throughout our lives, no matter where we were born. When we grow up, we can uproot ourselves, move around, and make changes, if even on a small scale. If we acquire the skills, we can decide who we become no matter where we come from.

As we grow and mature, we begin to observe the natural cycle that resides within us all. It's as unique to us as is our fingerprint, and when we befriend it, we can relax into the rhythm of it. Our life's winters allow us introspection. As we hibernate and rest, we discover the lessons from the previous season. When we are rested, we enter the spring of life. It brings hope for growth, energy, and productivity and invites us to discover another layer of our inner glory. The summers of our lives allow us to root ourselves more solidly in our new self-discoveries, and when we are ready, we start letting go of what no longer fits the new person we have become. Our lives' Autumns arrive to cleanse us from distractions and anything that might sabotage our newly found growth. And then it's time for introspection again.

After several seasonal cycles, we, as people, mature. As we mature, our lives begin to bear fruit. Our fruit reflects the place we decided to root ourselves into. If we were lucky and happened to land in fertile ground with plenty of shelter and other resources, we may grow too quickly. The wind may bend us to a breaking point because we didn't have to weather the storms of life. Or, we may have been born in punishing conditions, having to fight for every piece of nourishment and every drop of water, and struggle is all we know. While this makes hardy trees, the environment may produce less impressive-looking fruit. Wherever you come from, my dear friend, you can start changing it. You can edge closer and closer to more fertile ground or challenge yourself by moving toward the turbulence of life. This book is a reminder that if we focus on our own journey and make the most of it, we can live a meaningful, joyous, and compassionate life. By focusing on our own journey of becoming, we can stay present with our lives, goals, loved ones, and spiritual connection. In essence, how we live our lives directly affects the world we leave behind for future generations.

Writing this book took me five years because I needed time to heal and mature into a more precise and effective communicator. In 2017, I was still hiding from a dangerous stalker, unaware of a stress-induced brain injury, all the while trying to manage everyday life and keep my mentoring business going. Even with a secured publishing deal, I wasn't ready to share. And I didn't feel safe to share.

Had I written this book back then, I would have shared from a place of exhaustion and impatience. In essence, the last five years have served me well in helping me heal and mature. The time I claimed for my recovery helped me get clear on how I want to express myself through the pages of this book and what magic I want to create together with you, my dear reader.

Don't get me wrong. I haven't somehow "arrived" at being perfect or thinking there's nothing more for me to learn. I know that as this cycle ends, another one begins, and I'll be a beginner once more. As a life-long learner, I will continue to grow and evolve until my last breath.

By sharing my continuing journey with you, I want to highlight how persistent hope and intentional action can create a brighter future. I'm also here to remind you of your undeniable inner power, no matter how deep life's storms may have buried it. Even if your current circumstances are wrecking you, I hope that this book can give your inner thoughts a safe harbor so that you can begin to rest and nourish yourself.

I see the power within you, even if you can't see it yet, and it is my greatest pleasure to remind you of that power throughout this journey. I hope that you will enjoy our time together and expect that we laugh, cry, and fortify our wisdom together. Yes, this book is about me: a frightened little girl fighting for her dignity in the dark forest of people-pleasing and trauma, and I am honored that you have chosen to walk this journey with me. But I also encourage you to reflect my words onto your own life. Where we end up, I'm not sure. But I trust that our journey together will catalyze you to remember that **you are - in fact - the star of YOUR story**!

Hunter Valley,
NSW, Australia
October, 2023

CONTENTS

PART IV: The Deep Well

PART V: Home

INTRODUCTION

When I was a little girl, around five years old, my uncle sat me up on a massive horse named Donut. As I ran my fingers through his light brown mane and sensed the hypnotic scent of horses in the summer, I discovered for the first time how it felt to be safe.

My very first safe space was with Donut.

Funny, isn't it? What we find safe. High on this massive Finnish draft horse, I should have been scared, but I wasn't. You see, up there, nothing could reach me. No pain, hatred, abuse, or drunken vitriol could get me. At that moment, there was nothing but my connection with this horse who could easily hurt me but - I believed - never would.

That was the first time in my brief life that I had felt free from my father's abuse: alcoholism, narcissism, and neglect. In twelve hours, my life had turned on a penny. The night before, I had hidden in a potato cellar under hessian bags to escape two grown, drunken men - acquaintances of my father - looking to brutalize me by stealing the only thing I truly owned: my innocence.

Can you imagine going from such terror to such a sense of safety in a matter of hours? Aren't kids brave? Should they *have* to be? For a long time, I felt victimized by my father's lack of protection, and for a good reason. His prioritizing of his addiction, lack of compassion, and neglectful parenting nearly caused me to be the victim of one of the most unimaginable acts in the world.

But, as many children do, I quickly moved on from the terrors of the night. As the daylight crept above the horizon, so did the promise of a brighter tomorrow. My father told me to get in the car because we would soon leave the unfamiliar house of horrors. While the thought of getting in the car with him meant that I would sit in the stench of his now familiar, disgusting hangover halitosis, I couldn't wait to leave. I wasn't sure if I was agitated because I wanted to run away from what had happened the night before or I was keen to leave because my father told me we would go horse riding. Honestly, it didn't matter to me. I just wanted to get out of this unsafe house full of strangers.

Within those twelve hours, my tender child's body climbed from the darkness of a damp potato cellar to sitting high on a powerful and majestic horse. Both Donut and I were basking in the gentle summer morning sun of Northern Savo, Finland. Those twelve hours showed me that life is dichotomous. I didn't have the words to express it, and I certainly had never even heard the word dichotomous. I was five. But I learned what this feeling meant: that one minute, life could be complicated and dangerous, and the next, it could be calm, safe, and liberating.

Growing up with narcissistic parental influence made me adaptable. Life felt like an ocean, sometimes calm and sometimes stormy, but always a force of its own. Sometimes, the changing moods came at me faster than I could process, and black-and-white, rigid thinking would not keep me safe. Life wasn't fair, and there was nothing I could do about it. Nothing felt certain, so I had to learn to embrace change. At first, moving within the shades of gray felt clumsy, but over time and with many repetitions, I became fluent in surfing the unpredictable waves of my father's changing moods.

Yes, I had become skilled at navigating the ebbs and flows of life, but there were times when I continued to nearly drown in the riptides of my father's rage. I had learned to live in a form of hyper-vigilance that caused me psychoemotional distress but would - at least - keep me physically safe.

It took me years to overcome the anxiety I had learned to live with. The process was arduous and complex and could not be bypassed. I would not heal until I was ready to embrace two separate realities: my trauma reality and the non-trauma world around me. Even when others were trying to help me, there were times I didn't recognize it. Imagine being fully caught in the undercurrent of trauma and seeing something swimming in the waves right in front of you. Our traumatized self may see a shark, where a non-traumatized person may see a lifejacket. Our subjective pain and readiness to heal dictates what we see in any given situation.

But sometimes, we are too tired even to take the time to look. Some of us have been so jaded by the world and the abuse we have experienced that it can be hard to have hope. The challenge then is: if I give up on hope, do I give up on life? When you hit rock bottom, you realize that there is only one person in the world who can save you: **You**.

Many of my highly traumatized students protest this notion, and I get it. When you've been so used to fighting for everything, at some point, you just want to give up. But when I remind them of the light that is still within them, and we begin to take small steps in restoring hope, my students' lives transform from what looks like a dead-end to a curious intersection.

When the student is ready, I ask them: "Where in your life do you have a safe space, person, or situation that you swim to when the waves of your life become unmanageable?" Once they nominate an entity, I ask them: "When you reach that space of safety, for right then, just for that moment, can you let go of the terror lingering within you? For that moment, can you feel safe?".

Donut was my life jacket. Thank heavens I swam to him. In that one interaction, he taught me that no matter what I was going through, I could let go of the past pain and relax into the meaningful moment right now.

You might exclaim, "Youthful folly!" and you may are right. I would also argue that sometimes, naïveté can help us get through hard times. And sometimes, being silly can help us relax. As you may know, our sense of safety is strongly connected with our capacity to relax. So, no matter how anxious you feel right now, my questions to you are:

1. Who are the people you can relax around?
2. Who makes you laugh?
3. What hobby or location is your "happy place"?
4. What tangible thing, situation, relationship, or symbolic item makes you feel comfortable and safe, and
5. What does the symbolism in your life mean to you sincerely at your core?

Highly intuitive people would argue that everything means something. Sometimes, assigning meaning is easy. A wedding ring, a mother, or a first ride on your new horse can all be meaningful parts of your life. But there's a flip side to the meaning-making power of intuition. Because everything tends to mean something, arranging things, relationships, symbols, and people into an order of importance can be tricky.

Many thriving in the sensory world argue that assigning deep meaning to everything is a fool's errand. They can easily arrange items, relationships, situations, and people into clear categories of importance simply by their utility and proximation. But, overlooking meaning deeper than practicality may lessen life's profound context and nuance. Taking a moment to appreciate the symbolism of life while not getting bogged down by it brings about an abundant life of meaning, clarity, and connection.

Whatever intensity you prefer for assigning meaning, at some point, you experience a noteworthy occurrence, as I did with Donut. You recognize the incident as meaningful because it awakened something fundamental in you. But Donut didn't only teach me how to assign meaning to life's activities. He also showed me how to assign value. Yes, my interaction with him was meaningful, but it was also invaluable. This distinction was important to me because it helped this powerless little girl who had been too scared to enter the terrible twos to start assigning value on herself, even if in a very passive way.

You see, when **you** place value on something, **you automatically place significance in yourself** as the evaluator of that thing. Simply having an opinion on something makes you an authority in your own life. As a child with a narcissistic parental wound, I had a lot to learn about self-establishment and self-authority. Like many children of narcissistic parents, I had gotten used to only playing the role of a side character in my father's life. I had become so conditioned to think of him first that I didn't recognize any of my own likes and dislikes. But Donut helped me see myself as a real person. Instead of always looking to someone else for guidance or evaluation, Donut helped me learn to decipher for myself what was important for me and what was not.

I doubt anyone placed the same value on my experience with Donut as I did. For my father, taking me horse riding was likely just a distraction, an alibi, or another opportunity to party. Or perhaps that's too harsh. But I would bet my hard-earned money on the fact that the meaning for him was something entirely different than it was for me. But you know what? I'm going to set a boundary with myself here.

I don't want to spend an extraordinary amount of time dissecting his agenda for that day. The bottom line is that I don't know and have no way of finding out. What I can do is bring attention back to what I learned and what I may need as I navigate these painful memories.

It's easy to waste time wondering about others' behavior, agendas, or feelings, but I'd like to remind you to put on your own life vest first. In other words, I invite you to focus on yourself and begin to claim your power before attempting to understand those who have hurt you. As long as you don't feel empowered within yourself, it's almost impossible to see anyone else's experience in a balanced and productive way. So, let's focus on you. What is meaningful for you? What makes you feel safe?

Like it did for me, your meaningful occurrences can help you determine your values, needs, and wants in life. They can also help you discover a baseline of safety and security in life. When something feels meaningful, ask yourself: "What feels significant in this situation?" Then, take some time to reflect on the significance, and how you may continue to increase or decrease its effects in your life.

You are the only person who determines what feels meaningful for you and in what way. Positive or negative. No-one else gets a vote. So, what is significant for you, and why?

My experience with Donut was meaningful for me. This 1400-pound horse was my first space of safety. I accepted Donut, and he received me. We saw one another, and anyone who knows horses knows they have a sixth sense about people. They seem to know precisely when a person really needs them. When a spiritual connection is established, our horses accept our vulnerability. Softly blowing air in our faces, they are able to breathe love into our souls when we most need it.

As you can imagine, that interaction with Donut has influenced my whole life, from healing to self-mastery. It has validated me in a way that only a child of a narcissistic parent can yearn for. It helped me understand my values, needs and wants in a powerful way and gave me my first space of safety so that I could begin to heal and discover the light within me.

Donut helped me establish a core sense of security and inner strength. He showed me how quickly circumstances can change if I stay present with life. He showed me that I was a powerful being and that whatever was going on in my life, I had some capacity to change it for the better. To this day, whenever I'm having a bad day and fall short of who I aspire to be, his reflection of my true, empowered self rings in my ears: "Remember who you are."

The discovery of my authentic self began with Donut, and it has morphed into something a child with my experiences could never have imagined. That one interaction, when I was only five years old, changed my life's trajectory and how I saw myself. That one interaction planted a seed of transformation from an abused child to an empowered woman. But of course, I didn't know it at the time. I find that our best insights come after we've lived through enough contemplative winters of life.

Looking back to this pivotal experience, I recognize that Donut didn't only help me. Through my work, his grace has been passed on to my students as I hold a safe space for them to discover their core sense of self. It's as if the light from that day has followed me across continents, careers, relationships, and into my purposeful life. Donut's gift of light has been passed on through me to my friends, students, and their loved ones, and it continues to guide me as I do my part in creating a more joyous, compassionate, creative, and effective world.

I've lived in four different countries, made friends everywhere, found true love, and healed from my painful past to discover my greatest gifts to the world. I have run empowerment workshops, written courses on personal integration, and built successful businesses making money doing something I love. Despite my childhood trauma, I have learned to open my heart to global service. All this, and my online safe house, Sumiloff Academy of Human Integration, is a significant product of the love and light Donut catalyzed within me that day. I am paying forward the gift a Finnish draught horse gelding gave me when I was young and vulnerable: My first safe space.

This book is written as an homage to the safe spaces I have been given and those I have created. Safe spaces are imperative for our healing, development, and self-mastery. Without them, we can't rest, recover, mature, and learn new ways of being.

Establishing safe spaces around us starts from within and expands outward. By discovering the safety within ourselves, we can begin to offer it to others. If we are intentional, together, we can create a safer world by integrating ourselves and then showing up authentically for others. No more power games out of fear. No more predatory behavior because we realize that cooperation brings better overall results than competition.

As you walk this journey with me, I hope you begin or continue your own personal pilgrimage. I invite you to take this book into the privacy of your own mind, hopes, and dreams as you journey through your emotional landscape and unveil your inner greatness.

I wrote this book as a safe space for you. While most of it talks about my journey of healing and development, I have included some questions for you as well. I wanted to make the most of our journey together by asking questions that drill into the heart of the matter. But you get to choose how deep you go, and if anything I have written feels threatening, upsetting, or otherwise irrelevant to you, feel free to skip ahead or just pace yourself through those sections.

Thank you for joining me on this journey from a scared little girl to a master mentor of personal empowerment. I appreciate you.

Part 1

THE HORSE GIRL

Chapter 1

PUTTING MY PAIN TO WORK

"Underneath my deepest wounds
lay my greatest gifts to the world."

- MERJA SUMILOFF

I WAS HAVING A DEEP CONVERSATION with a close friend over coffee. I had just told them everything I could remember about my childhood trauma. I haven't shared most of it in this book or out there in public because I am not ready to talk about all of it. But in private, such tender conversations with trusted few have helped me reflect on my life in a deep way. I often get asked: "How could someone like you break the spell of such fundamental wounding and childhood abuse and come to live their life on your own terms?" My short answer: Instead of letting my pain rule my world, I put my pain to work for me.

Was it easy? Not at all. It took years of learning, practicing, and performing new skills that people growing up in loving households take for granted. It took stubborn determination to keep going when common sense would tell you to stop. It took unbelievable courage to stay with my pain when it spoke about its most harrowing misconceptions dressed up as "truths". It took years of reparenting myself to get to point zero. And it was totally worth it.

Many of us feel like the cards we were dealt in life hold us back from living a purposeful life. You may be experiencing systemic discrimination, you may be in the process of recovering from trauma, be stuck in a job that doesn't nourish your soul, or be utterly confused about what you "should" be doing with your life. I see so many people struggling with the existential question of "to be, or not to be, and what to be?"

In my early adulthood years, I have to admit that I didn't put much thought into building a purposeful life and even less effort into how I could make my past pain work for me. I lived my life as it unfolded and never tried to force it. I was just happy to be alive, and relatively safe. I only started examining my life's trajectory when Peter Hagerty, my partner and the top Purpose and Authenticity Coach in the world, explained to me that purpose is not something you do. It's a journey of becoming.

I came to understand that our purpose is not a job but the expression and action inspired by our unique human drives. Our values, as well as our original thoughts, feelings, intuitive flashes, and senses, can guide us to stay on our purposeful journey. In other words, your purpose can stay the same, even if your jobs take different forms.

Hagerty describes the purpose path as a spiral around our authentic being. His work shows us that while chargeless, massless, spaceless, and timeless and that these elements combined make it formless, our purpose takes a concrete form in the outside world through our inspired action. In effect, our purpose is an element of ourselves we feel called to explore, express, and build a life around. Our purpose, thus, is a persisting theme or a motivating factor we cannot shed.

For as long as I can remember, I've yearned to help others. I've been a coach since the age of sixteen because sports teams, individuals, and companies have identified the value of this drive within me. I remember once being asked: "If you could do anything, what would you do?" My response surprised even me.

"I want to take calls from people who need help - and then help them! I want to run a help desk for a happy and meaningful life."

When I had the opportunity to work with Peter, my purpose path started lighting up. Helping people felt like an original thought percolating deep within my authentic being. But I doubted myself. With the gaslighting I had received as a child, I was still struggling to know what thoughts were my own, and what were conditioning. Surely, I was simply conditioned to help others.

As so many children of narcissistic parental wounding do, I continued marginalizing my inner guidance. I decided there was supposed to be more to my purpose than just helping others. When I started looking for patterns of what had been driving me in the past, an overwhelming sense of confusion came upon me. It seemed like I felt most joyous when I was supporting others. It didn't feel like a trauma response but a genuine drive to accomplish goals with other people. I was wholly confused and started to panic. "It's ok," Peter said. "Start from where you are."

I was stuck in rigidly believing that our purpose had to only originate from inspiration and that our past traumatic experiences merely stood in the way of our success. I remembered all the conversations I'd had with therapists encouraging me to find my own path beyond helping others, but I just couldn't. It wasn't until I decided to follow my inner voice that I realized something fundamental: My trauma was connected to my purpose. I concluded that instead of being inspired to take action, I had been moved by what I didn't want.

I didn't want to feel unsafe. I didn't want to be marginalized. I didn't want to be abused or alone. *And most of all, I didn't want anyone else to feel unsafe, marginalized, abused, or lonely in my presence.* At that moment, when I stopped trying to control my pain, I finally landed on something I **wanted**. I wanted to pay Donut's kindness and powerfully healing presence forward.

When I spoke to Peter about not trusting my quiet inner voice and instead listening to others when they told me that my helping was a trauma response, he was not surprised. He told me that our purpose path can, and often does, intertwine with our experiences with trauma. There and then, I realized something very powerful:

1. My inner voice telling me that supporting others in a meaningful way toward a common goal was, in fact, arising from my inspired self and
2. That our trauma can undoubtedly expose and energize our purpose.

Throughout this process, I realized that two seemingly opposing perspectives could both be valid and valuable in their own ways. With Peter's help, I came to understand that my greatest gift to the world - *helping those who have been dealt a bad hand in life to take back their power and live a meaningful life* - lies underneath the pain of my own life experiences.

From thereon, I was able to see my trauma a little differently. Of course, each child deserves to grow up in a loving and healthy home. I do not intend to glorify traumatic life events in any way. Working on my purposeful life taught me that my past experiences weren't only something negative. I came to realize that what had happened to me was not entirely in vain.

The trauma I experienced enabled me to fully engage with my purposeful path of supporting others. The trauma did not cause me to want to help people, but it did teach me how to support them.

Chapter 2

WE'RE NEVER ON THE WRONG PATH

"A good mentor hopes you will move on.
A great mentor knows you will."

- LESLIE HIGGINS
(CHARACTER IN TV SERIES TED LASSO)

*D*ONUT WAS MY FIRST LOVE. He had taken a vulnerable little girl and made her feel safe and seen shortly after one of the most traumatic events of her brief life. As a result, I felt a strong kinship with horses. One that I knew would be there for the rest of my life. Unsurprisingly, and for the longest time, I thought that my life's purpose was to work with horses.

While still in school, I was horse-mad. To be fair, like in many religious experiences, being with horses breathed life into my heart and motivation into my soul. I would work every free hour to raise money to afford a riding lesson or attend a riding summer camp. I worked hard, I helped where I could, and none of it felt like a compromise. I never complained about the long days, even if I didn't get paid or wasn't allowed to ride. Just being around horses was enough for me.

My friend Kikka was fortunate to have weekly riding lessons, and I would go with her as often as possible. No weather was too treacherous, not rain, not even the freezing cold of Finnish winters. I was clear on my mission: I was there to watch her and the other pupils ride and learn everything I could. And if I could support my friend in any way, I would. I wanted to be there even if I couldn't ride because it wasn't about sitting on a horse and bossing him around. It was about learning - whichever way I could - with my friend.

Interacting with horses had become my spiritual practice. After finishing secondary education, I calmly and firmly transitioned into my first occupation: horse husbandry. For my third level of education, I comfortably slipped into studying agriculture and equine science. I remember my mother asking if it was what I wanted, and my gut said "yes" without hesitation.

Mum knew not to argue. She was a fair and insightful woman who did what she could to support me. The years I had spent making money and spectating my friend's riding lessons convinced her of my commitment to the equestrian life. She knew being with horses made me happy, and that was enough for her. I studied and worked hard and felt free and purposeful after graduation. I finally got to do what I always wanted: spend all my days and hours with horses and get paid for it!

In my first job, I had the privilege of working in the most prestigious riding school in Finland, Keskustalli. Piiu and Pertti Paloheimo gave me every opportunity to learn and solidify my craft. When it was time for me to move on, I was sad to leave what had become my professional family.

The Paloheimos were those great mentors who embraced me throughout my employment and supported me when I moved on. From Helsinki, I moved to Ireland to continue building my equestrian experience. I was still living my childhood dream, and I remember thinking that I was on purpose.

I worked hard, and within three months, I had proven my mettle. I became the head groom of one of Europe's most prestigious showjumping yards, the Waterside Stud. The only thing I was still yearning for was to compete at the highest level myself. The naïveté of childhood dreams can be delusional but also very powerful. I could see only one road ahead: representing my country in the Olympics.

Ten years later, I had a string of my own young competition horses and a rented yard in South County Dublin. At that time, I was still convinced that my purpose was working with horses, but I was about to learn that horses were just the lightning rod for me. They were a stepping stone to a world where I would be helping others take back their personal power and live a meaningful life.

Chapter 3

THE OCCASIONAL TORMENTOR

"Life has a great way of reminding
us that we can't control the winds,
but that we can steer our ship."

- MERJA SUMILOFF

I WAS CRUISING ALONG WHEN IT all came crashing down. My top horse, Vesper, one of the most generous horses I've ever known, injured herself in the paddock. While she survived her injury and was pain-free after her recovery, I knew she would never be able to compete at the highest levels.

Before she got injured, my time competing with Vesper culminated at one of Europe's most significant equestrian events, the Dublin Horse Show, where we achieved two 3rd placings.

For the longest time, I blamed myself, even though it was just a freak accident and not preventable. I mean, what's the definition of disempowerment? It is to accept liability for something you have no power over. I had no control over Vesper's injury, but I still felt it was my fault.

Back then, I wasn't able to handle the setback. I froze. I had been on a winning streak with horses, and nothing had ever really gone wrong for me. I didn't know how to take a disappointment seriously without taking it personally. I made everything about myself while making sure to give Vesper all the veterinary care she needed.

When I accepted that Vesper's career was over, I spent months agonizing about how I had let her down and how I should have been able to control the uncontrollable. I allowed my toxic ego to torment me with messages of inadequacy. In the meantime,

Vesper was becoming pain-free and no longer had the pressure to perform. She was happy.

Has that ever happened to you? Have you ever taken responsibility for something you had no control over? Have you obsessed over the uncontrollable?

Although I could see Vesper happy in her retirement, I kept tormenting myself. A voice in my head told me that *I had caused her pain and that I should be ashamed.* I had no idea where the voice was coming from at the time, but I would soon find out. What hurt me the most was my harsh inner dialogue and my debilitating, unregulated empathy for everyone. Well, everyone, except for me.

Therapists and trusted colleagues have often told me that I have too much compassion and empathy for others. They quickly remind me that this is a common challenge within the narcissistic parental abuse dynamic. Ultimately, I am programmed to only feel empathy for others and never for myself. I have come to understand and accept that this kind of imbalanced compassion comes with a price.

The cost is the pain I feel with and sometimes on behalf of others. At times, it doesn't even matter whether *they* feel it or not. Someone, like in this instance Vesper, could be completely pain-free, and I would project onto them the pain *I feared they were experiencing.* This kind of empathy was my hangover from the gaslighting I experienced as a child. It is toxic and purposeless.

I was stuck believing that Vesper was still in pain, even though her pain management had been successful and she had healed fully. My problem was that I held onto the misguided beliefs of my conditioning. Despite any factual evidence, I was convinced that my neglect had caused her injury. Like a child told that her father's misery in life was her fault, I assumed responsibility. Sure, her competitive career was over, but she didn't care! It was I who was unable to let go of her injury. I was the one causing the unnecessary suffering within me.

Because of my divine friendship and connection with Vesper - and my inability to handle this setback - I was convinced that my competition career was also over. Like a petulant child, I completely overlooked the other young horses in their stables and convinced myself that my purpose had fallen apart. It may seem like an overreaction, and that's how it looks to me now. But I also have compassion toward my younger self. How I saw it at the time was that I had failed to look after horses in the way that they had looked after me.

Oh, how much I beat myself up for that. Because I couldn't fix Vesper, I shamed myself into trying to fix people around me. My toxic ego kept telling me I only had value by rescuing others. So, I listened to my noxious pride and started rescuing animals and even friends by the dozen. Then, I got overwhelmed. Years later, I realized I was rescuing animals to avoid my feelings of powerlessness. I wanted to be the hero I had failed to be for Vesper. It took a literal kick in the head by one of my rescue horses to see that my life had become unsustainable and that I was barreling toward destruction.

I had to quiet my toxic ego and let others have the right to their own experiences. I had to stop interpreting others' situations as worse than they were and cease projecting my own insecurities onto them. I had to grow up and realize that not everything is about me. I finally understood that if I didn't heal my childhood wounds, I would continue to show up in life dressed up as an adult but thinking, feeling, and behaving like a little kid.

This slice of humble pie was more bitter than too much lemon rind in a cheesecake. To truly respect others around me meant that I had to learn new skills. I had to learn to feel comfortable in the discomfort of others' pain. I had to learn to ask questions and not to assume. Others had the right to be, feel, think, and express themselves independently and authentically without my interference disguised as "helping."

Like everything unhealthy in life, breaking my childlike urge to fix others came with a silver lining. Although I was not aware of it back then, it put me squarely back on my purpose path. Once I realized the sabotage I was causing in my relationships, I started listening more than talking. I asked others thoughtful questions to find out what was really going on for them. I heard others' unspoken words and recognized their non-verbal communication for the first time. I felt more connected with others and started examining the drive behind my behavior. I decided to sign up for therapy and hire a healing mentor, so that I could heal myself, and support others in a way that was right for them.

With the support of my newly hired team, I was able to create more respectful relationships with my horses and the people around me. I dove deeply into my personal healing and development journey, which felt completely natural to me. My capacity to stay with the "ugly feelings" made me the master mentor I am today. I was able to take my pain and healing, and make sense of it for others on a similar life path.

Having the humility to ask for help, heal, and connect authentically with others wasn't easy, but it was worth the challenge. Pain, when resolved, has the power to bring about the healing and resurrection of a better version of ourselves. Extreme pain, when resolved, brings about a new, more authentic version of ourselves. A version that allows us to show up in life with more purpose and grace.

Ultimately, Vesper's injury taught me that my purpose was not to *rescue anyone*. It was to support those who needed *and wanted* my support. Having Vesper in my life led me to listen to people's actual needs, not my toxic ego's interpretation of them.

Vesper also taught me that my - and her - purpose had not failed just because one career path had ended. Her injury showed me what a purposeful pivot looked like. Her noble and tender heart taught me that it was okay to change the course of our lives and that new opportunities will arise when things don't go as expected. Of course, these insights weren't instantaneous. They took years to become conscious and actualize.

Alongside my therapist and mentor, Vesper had become one of the most valued teachers in my life. Yes, occasionally, the role of a mentor is to be a tormentor, and some of these lessons were painful. In time, the devastation of her injury turned into a piece of wisdom I will always treasure: **You can't control life, but you can steer your boat. If you try to control everything that goes on around you, you may miss out on the unique gifts life has in store for you.** Vesper went on to have a foal and a wonderful retirement.

Like Vesper, every horse I have owned has offered me something special: a reminder of the crack of vulnerability in my soul that lets the light of inspiration in. The equine aura was my continuous safe zone, especially when connecting with humans was too painful. Even though my drive to compete disappeared with Vesper's injury, horses have continued to be a massive part of my purpose path. They have continued to teach me about life and increase my personal growth and psychological well-being.

Because I now understand that there is a purpose behind every joyous and painful experience, I can step back from my immediate reaction, be patient, and allow myself to see everything more clearly. I now have the power to keep learning and pivoting. Life experiences, even if negative, are essential. They teach us the lessons we need to know to understand ourselves more deeply, advance in life, and fully become all we can be.

My pain gave me the insight, the drive, and the capacity to support others through their struggles. It has been the most incredible privilege of my life to help others find the gifts that lie beneath their deepest wounds. So, let us not be afraid of the torment of life. Instead, let's find the meaning in the pain so that we can learn the lessons and live fully.

What is your pain trying to tell you?

Chapter 4

THE MEANING OF PAIN

"I can bear any pain as long
as it has meaning."

- HARUKI MURAKAMI

THE MEANING OF OUR PAIN is assigned by us, the people around us, and society at large. There are as many responses to pain and victimization as there are people. After all, while pain is a shared experience within humankind, our understanding of pain is individual to our own.

Some are quick to point the finger at the victim: "You would not have been hit if you had only kept your mouth shut" or "When you dress like that, you have no one else to blame if you get attacked." This kind of victim-blaming marginalizes the already injured party. It has the destructive power to re-traumatize us well beyond the original hurt.

Think about the old adage "adding insult to injury." This saying is a literal expression of how normalized victim blaming is. Many think that telling wounded people what they "should" have done differently will help them heal or keep them safe in the future. But this approach is like telling someone with a broken leg to walk it off. A broken leg, like a fractured mind or emotional injury, takes time and nurturing to heal. When we see that someone is in pain, we have some options. We can choose to be a part of their healing process, ignore them, or we can choose to continue injuring them with undermining words and actions.

Relying on others to help us heal is not the best course of action. I find that our friends, even the most trusted ones, can't always be there or offer the kind of support we need. According to my data from hundreds of student interviews, the most predictable way to heal is to take ownership of your own healing journey. As I was conducting these interviews, another interesting pattern arose: Choosing to work through our trauma helps us make meaningful discoveries.

The data showed that if we decide to heal ourselves, we can discover the purpose of our pain. Vesper's injury changed my career trajectory and, subsequently, my life. When I took time to reflect on what happened and why, it all started making sense. I didn't need to be a competition rider to continue on my purposeful path. Whether I competed or not, horses would continue to be an important part of my life, and my process of healing. Their incredible capacity to mirror my emotional landscape back to me taught me self-compassion as I continued to mend myself.

I learned that proactively claiming your time to heal helps you resolve any current pain and avoid getting hurt again in the future. When you proclaim your time to heal, you declare your worth as an individual. This act of self-governing starts an upward spiral of empowerment in our lives. When we prioritize our healing, we begin to respect ourselves more. When we respect ourselves more, we continue to prioritize ourselves. After several cycles, a helix of personal power is formed, and we begin to feel stronger in every area of our lives.

It's almost like we must learn this for ourselves before fully supporting others. Many well-meaning people have told domestic abuse victims to leave their relationship, thinking that the meaning they assign to another person's situation will empower them to leave. If you have ever been in these situations, you know how hard it can be to leave. The abuse is not just physical; it has most likely been emotional and psychological, too. Maybe even sexual and financial. The abuse often drains the victim of resources, personal sovereignty, and dignity. If the victim does not see or cannot imagine themselves as a separate physical, financial, and emotional entity from their abuser, they are unable to leave.

By claiming their time to heal and giving themselves what they need, survivors of domestic abuse can regain their dignity and become better equipped to change their circumstances. But if you know a person in a domestic abuse situation you know that most of this strengthening work has to be done in the privacy of the individual's mind first. Taking action in the outside world before you are ready to leave can only subject the victim to more abuse. You see, it's not about giving one-line solutions to complicated problems. Time does not heal all wounds. It's what you do - and how you do it - during that time that has the power to change your situation.

Complex situations need a 360-degree approach and a solid exit strategy. When you take the time to work through your past pain, you begin to see yourself more clearly. You are deserving; no matter what anyone has said to you before, self-prioritization shows you through action that you are important. If your resources are drained, do what you can. I know it won't be easy, and I personally know how impossible it may feel. But if you can, ask for the kind of help that will empower you to change your circumstances.

Another, unfortunately, common way to deal with trauma is using toxic positivity to minimize pain. When we think that pain is only bad, we assign a meaning of threat to painful experiences. This threat can make us hide and not face the hurt deep inside us. Just as victim-blaming does not work for healing, toxic positivity does not help us discover the purpose behind our pain. Pretending everything is okay will not help you learn the critical life insight that pain and the subsequent healing process have to offer.

Jumping to conclusions without taking the time to introspect is also unhelpful. Think about a stranger looking at your situation and, without asking any questions, offering their opinion. Is it likely that they know what you need? Unless they are highly intuitive and sensitive to others' needs, it's improbable that they know how to help you.

After Vesper got injured, some people told me it wasn't a big deal and that I should simply move on to another horse. While I probably swung all the way to the opposite extreme on the scale between self-loathing and toxic positivity, I'm glad I faced the pain head-on. I would have delayed discovering the meaning behind my pain. If we don't face life's difficulties directly, they'll come back to haunt us in another form. We can run, but we can't hide.

Meaning in our pain becomes more apparent as we step into the healing process. For some, the clarity arrives during the process itself, but for most, the lesson only becomes evident after the fact. **It can be hard to see the purpose of our pain while we are still in it.** It's like trying to find the woods within the trees.

Finding the meaning in our pain can take healing, distance, and adopting new and powerful habits. I know I'm ready to receive the meaning behind my painful experiences when I:

1. Get bored, angry, or uncomfortable with being a victim and want to take action.
2. Engage with people I trust and respect, and ask them some critical questions. Not defensive, passive-aggressive questions to justify my pain, but earnest questions such as:
   a. What information or facts may I not have about this situation?
   b. What effect could this situation have on others that are involved?
   c. When a similar situation happened to me before, how did I seem to deal with it?
   d. What needs within me are being overlooked?

When I feel angry or want to speak to others about my pain, I know I have started healing. When I ask meaningful, earnest questions about my situation, I can discover something new about myself. At the same time, I have learned to protect my unique process of healing. To stay on track, I **must** keep those engaging in victim-blaming and toxic positivity at arm's length. I am simply not prepared to halt my healing or remain stuck in my pain for the comfort of others.

Most people find comfort in victim blaming and toxic positivity because these activities take the attention away from their own pain and fears. I don't judge these people because I understand that these "tools" are just coping mechanisms. While I don't blame them, I do set boundaries with them. When I'm healing, I can't afford to focus on others' coping mechanisms. If I do that, I will soon fall back into my own. Relying on our old habits will not help us heal and grow. They will keep us trapped in pain for as long as we continue to revert back to them.

I have learned that allowing others to intervene or outright dictate my healing journey will not help me find the purpose of my pain. At best, it will steer me to the wrong conclusion, and at worst, it can re-traumatize me. Running away from our pain delays our healing and growth.

You see, **our pain is not who we are.** Our pain, even when overwhelming, is a shadow of a past that we continue to carry. Yes, our parents may have taught us that we have no value. But just because they taught us that does not make it universally true. Our pain can also be used as a source of fuel. There's nothing quite like sticking it to the haters, or working through a difficult situation just to prove the nay-sayers wrong. Learning to stay with our pain and observe it can help us look at it from different perspectives. Taking the time to observe your pain may even surprise you. As I did, you may discover a hidden positive drive in your trauma.

When we stop seeing pain as **only** "bad", and ourselves as **only** victims of our past, we can enter a new paradigm. When I stopped staring at my pain and put it to work for me, I met my partner, transformed my career, and moved across the world. I met people whom I still call my ride-or-die friends. Letting go of my conditioning of being a victim showed me that my pain had both positives and negatives attached to it.

Was it easy to let go of the label of "victim"? No. But I knew living a life of pain and unhappiness would be much harder. So, I decided to reclaim myself.

Chapter 5

RECLAIMING YOURSELF

"Reclaiming yourself is
the only investment
that will make your soul feel rich."

- MERJA SUMILOFF

CHANGE IS UNCOMFORTABLE. IT'S PAINFUL for the person changing and awkward for those around them. When one person in a relationship changes or heals, it can be scary for the other. Changes can cause unnecessary friction on our relationships. If we don't communicate the changes with our spouse in a way that makes sense to them, the relationship can begin to break down.

Communicating your change to those important to you will ease their discomfort and keep them informed about your process. If you're anything like me, those I love are important to me, and I want to keep them up-to-date. Whenever I can, I communicate my process of evolution with kindness and consideration for how my change may affect them or their lives.

Initially, sharing your personal journey with a significant other can make you feel vulnerable. Especially if you have started growing apart, you may feel a reluctance to let them see the newly discovered, tender parts of you. But if you want to fight for the relationship, sharing the new version of yourself is necessary. It's up to you how much or little to share, and if you feel uncomfortable even with the thought of it, start by sharing something small.

Keeping your partner up-to-date on your changing inner world can put them at ease, and asking them to share their thoughts about your growth can considerably increase your shared level of intimacy and connection. Taking their feedback seriously without taking it personally can be challenging, but learning to do so is liberating. I noticed a profound change in my relationships when I upgraded my communication skills. But don't take my word for it. Try it for yourself. If you can normalize open communication about both of your needs, the relationship can improve in unimaginable ways.

However, it is good to note that not all relationships are safe for sharing. If your partner or friend has belittled your shares in the past, they may not be able to offer a safe space for you. If someone doesn't respect your boundaries after you have asked them to do so in a calm way, they are unlikely to be safe. Please use your judgment when choosing who does and does not have the right to witness and partake in your journey of growth.

When we find something that works for us, we want to see those we love also enjoy the benefits. It's human nature to want to encourage others to change. However, it's good to remember that everyone is on their own life trajectory and has authority over their own lives. Even if what you have learned would positively impact others, simply telling them to change may not motivate them to take action. If you take the time to share your experiences lovingly and with patience, it allows others to choose what's right for them and may even inspire them to take action for themselves.

We get into trouble when we demand that others must change. I have yet to meet a person who hasn't, at some point, projected their fear-based wants onto their partner. These unconscious projections of how our partners should behave begin to erode the purity of the shared connection.

If you find yourself in a relationship full of woes, it's good to acknowledge that you too may be projecting onto the other. Our past unhealed resentments and frustrations aim the flashlight of our focus on what the other person is doing "wrong." We may end up poisoning our thoughts and those we care about with our unresolved trauma. If we don't work through our past pain, we may bring it to our current relationship, unload it on our partner, and unintentionally make them responsible for something they had no part in creating.

Don't get me wrong. I would have been wholly justified never to recover from my past trauma, all of which I haven't shared in this book. I genuinely think those who know my past and love me would have tolerated my projections on them out of pure compassion. No one would have judged me for continuing to be the powerless little girl hiding in the potato cellar. I could easily have leaned into my trust issues and chosen them over others' attempts to love me. But I wanted to choose love. I wanted to learn how to reclaim my life so that I could stop carrying my pain and live every day through powerful intention.

Learning to look for and discover the lessons hidden within past pain takes time, patience, and self-advocacy. I can honestly say that reclaiming myself has been the hardest thing I've ever done, but it is also the best thing I've done for myself. Investing in my healing and learning new skills have yielded the dividends of insights, wisdom, and, ultimately, better decisions and relationships.

Throughout this book, you'll see how valuable this process has been for me. Every lesson I have learned has made my life better and more manageable. And it all results from taking my power back. Having reclaimed myself, I can no longer imagine living with the false fear-based premise that all men are predators and that I can't trust anyone. Had I continued to believe those things, I would have hurt not only myself but everyone around me as well.

So, I asserted my sovereignty and took the time to do my inner work. When I was ready, I started sharing my discoveries with those I cared for. As a result, each relationship that was mutually caring, improved. For the first time in my life, my heart was open, and I felt seen. Simultaneously, my relationships fell apart with those who were invested in me staying "in my place." Those who didn't want me to empower myself disappeared when I started setting loving boundaries.

Taking a step back from the process, and taking time to witness the powerful transformation of my life had secondary, unintended consequences. I began moving closer to my purpose of helping those who have been dealt a bad hand in life to take back their power and live a meaningful life. I had inadvertently inspired others to heal, too.

Friends, family members, and clients started asking me how they, too, could learn the lessons from their pain and move on to a more joyous life. I showed them what I had done while reminding them that their unique healing journey would likely differ from mine. Even in my wildest dreams, I could not have imagined the changes they experienced.

While I wasn't yet aware of my future as a master mentor, seeing that my pain had empowered me and helped others felt meaningful. There indeed was purpose in my pain beyond me.

Am I encouraging you to stay in an abusive relationship, no matter what? Absolutely not. Not in any form or under any circumstance. The first ideal step toward healing is to remove yourself from the abusive situation. If you currently live in an abusive environment, do what you can to escape it. Set up a support network that is removed from the dynamic of the abuse. You are worth it. You deserve a life that looks like you, not a life that your trauma dictated. Also, remember that simply removing yourself from a situation of abuse is not enough. If you don't take steps to heal, you'll continue to carry your pain wherever you go and recreate the abusive situation somewhere else and with someone else.

Once you have removed yourself from abuse, get help. Whatever support you need, could you find a way to get it? Don't take no for an answer. Find out what support your local council, or tribe may offer in your situation, or simply reach out to us at the Sumiloff Academy. In my experience, most trauma can be healed with appropriate protection, care, skill development, and encouragement. Get help so that you, too, can discover the purpose beyond past pain. You're worth it.

Stay away from any indoctrination that leads you back to the abusive situation. Some people or communities try to hide abuse to not look bad. It's wise to ask yourself if the input you are receiving is aimed at helping you heal or keeping you in line with the status quo.

You may have to cut ties with people you have loved and respected in the past because they are making excuses for the abuse or the abuser. Sometimes, the best support you can get is from a professional who doesn't know you or your situation personally.

Finally, give yourself time to heal. Extend grace to the incredible being that you are. The world needs you to be you, not aspire to some unrealistic standard or schedule. There's no "perfect" in healing, so don't compare yourself to others. Get help that is tailored for you, and simply keep going. What may seem like a different or imperfect healing journey may actually be perfect under the circumstances and, most importantly, perfect for YOU.

Being able to reclaim your power requires separating your past from this current moment and all the future possibilities. It also takes practice to remember that your past is not your present and doesn't have to determine your future.

If your abuse is in the past and you are safe now, you can get on with your lessons. Even if you struggle with parental narcissistic abuse, depression, PTS, PTSD, or C-PTSD, it is crucial to take a moment and consciously recognize that *right now*, you are safe.

Right now, you can move forward, even if only an inch. As an exercise to demonstrate this concept, I recommend my students pick an item that represents their painful past. It can be a book, a stone, or a piece of jewelry. Then, I show them how they can choose to put down the symbol of their pain, even for just a second.

Letting go of that item can initially be challenging. The longer you have carried the pain, the more familiar it feels. It may even feel like it's a part of you. You may think: "My pain has been a shield that has protected me for such a long time. Now I'm supposed just to let it go?! I don't think so!"

I am not suggesting you stop having boundaries or completely let go of your protective armor. I am asking, just for now, that you put down the pain you have carried with you and enjoy a moment of safety and painless existence. It can be a second, a minute, or an entire day. It doesn't matter. If you want to pick up the pain and carry it with you, you can. The choice is entirely yours; no one else can choose for you. You've put a lot of effort into coping with that painful past. You deserve a moment to at least catch your breath.

If you've had abusive experiences and reclaimed yourself despite them, you know that healing does not automatically excuse or forgive the abuse. I healed myself for **me**. Reclaiming myself from the narcissistic parental wound has been the best investment of my life. I reclaimed myself to get on with my life, not to let my abusers off the hook. I used every opportunity to find safe spaces so that I could continue to heal.

This Horse Girl made one sober decision at a time to show herself that life was precious and worth living.

Part II

THE WANDERER

Chapter 6

LEAVING HOME

"Not all those who wander are lost."

- J. R. R. TOLKIEN

ACCORDING TO THE UNITED NATIONS Population Division, in 2020, 3.6% of the world's population currently lives in a country that is not their own. People leave for many reasons. Some leave because they have to. War, famine, safety, and freedom from persecution force individuals and families to leave all they know behind and move to a new place. My Grandfather had to go. He was young when his whole family were uprooted from Karelia, a part of Finland that was lost to the Soviet Union in the Second World War.

These families had to move to stay within Finnish borders. When they landed in their new hometown, my Grandfather's traumatized family was painted with a brush that said "dirty Russian." Their Soviet-sounding name didn't help. Such was the hatred of "the invaders" back then.

I left Finland when I was twenty. In contrast to my Grandfather's experience, when I left home and landed at my destination, I was the exotic Scandinavian with every caricature that came with the label. Never mind the fact that Finland isn't even a part of Scandinavia. The contrast between my journey and that of my

Grandfather showed me that bias is in the eye of the beholder. We all see others through our assumptions of them.

Unlike those fleeing hostilities, I had the p-r-i-v-i-l-e-g-e of choosing to go. There was a big difference between my journey of exploration and that of my Grandfather, who was simply trying to stay alive. I could choose when and where I would go, whereas they were told to leave and assigned a destination.

I left because I knew, early on in my life, that I would not live in Finland forever. While I love my country and will always refer to it as "home," I knew I could not stay. Something was calling me to leave, and I wasn't sure what. Now, in hindsight, I left because I was destined to meet people, understand cultures, educate myself further, and create safe spaces around the world.

Through my process of leaving Finland, I made efforts to remember what my Grandfather had gone through. So, when I left, I vowed to make the most of my journey. *He had to leave,* whereas I was a wanderer, an explorer, and the world was my oyster.

Was my journey always a song and dance? No, of course not. But, I understood that my daily challenges were ones *I chose* because I had chosen to leave. My daily trials and tribulations were within my control. After all, I could always go back to Finland! The challenges I chose by leaving, for a big part, were inconveniences compared to those fleeing war or persecution.

Moving abroad - alone - opened my eyes. Firstly, I lost my entire practical support network and had to be willing to start over. When I moved to Ireland, I didn't know anyone there. I had the security of obtaining a job through a friend; her family owned my place of work and residence, but I did not know anyone in person. It was a terrifying experience - especially as a deeply introverted person - to present myself to a bunch of strangers for the first time. But you know what? It also felt freeing.

It felt like a clean-slate experience where I could leave behind all my old baggage and start anew. Looking back, I got an opportunity to begin a whole new stage of life. A flame of enthusiasm for an entirely new world was ignited in my soul. In this new world, I could decide who I was. Don't get me wrong; I wasn't running away from who I had been. It felt more like I wanted to shed the outgrown parts of my life that were no longer working for me.

I embraced the opportunity to reinvent myself and pondered, "Who do I want to be?" "Who am I with no projections from people who knew me in my past?" and "How do I want to show up in this new role I'm choosing?"

All of us have these clean-slate opportunities throughout our lives. When you start a new job, begin studying, or move to another town, you, too, get to define or reinvent who you are. But you don't have to change countries to ask yourself these questions. Every change in life presents you with a chance to start anew. Every day is an opportunity to build a life you love. You can wipe the slate clean each morning and do your best to redirect your thoughts and activities to ones that match the life you are creating.

The privileged many who travel or expatriate out of choice do it primarily because they want to feel free or explore all the world offers. This was the case for me. But even though I wanted to move abroad, leaving wasn't easy. Leaving the comfort of the known, friends, and family can be the hardest thing you'll ever do.

Even if you leave on your own terms, departing takes courage and perseverance. Some procrastinate about going or staying. I get it. I can tell you from my own experience that fear of change is a real thing. Once you leave, everything will be different. When you leave, the people who love and respect you either go with you or make all efforts to stay in touch. If your relationship ends because of relocation, it simply wasn't meant to be.

As human beings and mammals, it is normal for us to view change as threatening. We are literally hard-wired to stay with our tribe and what feels comfortable. One change can feel challenging but is usually manageable. But when the rate of change escalates, so does the need for the brain to adjust. Thus, two simultaneous changes may feel threatening, and three can feel outright fatal.

So, how do we deal with the threat of change? We seek comfort and familiarity. When everything around you feels out of control, you reach for the one thing - everyone has one - that will comfort you. It may be chocolate, exercise, wine, or video games. Reaching for these things offers us a temporary safe space.

This safe space can help us to relax, feel more in control, and help us integrate ourselves into the newly discovered reality. Sometimes, when our circumstances shift massively, we create new comfort habits to keep us going. Think about the new comfort habits you adopted during the lockdowns of the COVID-19 global pandemic. What were your primary ways of coping with the unknown future? Are those mechanisms ones that you would like to keep? Do they build a life that looks more like the authentic you? Are your comfort habits sabotaging you, or are they making you successful?

The unknown is scary, but we can prepare ourselves. Whether you adopt comfort habits to heal past trauma, reparent yourself, learn new life skills, or master your career, finances, or relationships, you get to commit to your success in the face of the unknown. The power to commit is yours.

Chapter 7

THE UNKNOWN

"People want progress, but
they don't want to change."

- EVA BURROWS

A PERSON'S INHERENT DIFFICULTY IN EMBRACING multiple changes simultaneously can leave them trapped in an unfulfilling life. We stay in unhealthy relationships, abusive jobs, and toxic places of residence because we are uncomfortable with the unknowns. Better the devil you know, right? As we stay in unstable or even dangerous situations, we make our lives more complicated than they need to be. We are conditioned to make the most out of a bad situation and avoid the discomfort of change.

Most people are not born with a positive attitude toward change. In fact, most of us must learn this skill later in life. Like most learning, the younger you are the more flexible your mind is. If you learn to embrace change as a child, by the time you're in your thirties, you have established a solid resilience and ability to face life's challenges. But you don't have to be young to learn this lesson. While learning may take a bit longer, it's very possible to adopt this worldview later in life if you go about it in a deliberate and well-thought-out way.

To get comfortable with change, we must learn the skills of patience and open-mindedness. We must be patient with ourselves as we learn to stretch our comfort zones. To extend our comfort zones, we must observe the positives that come from the unknown. In essence, we need to learn the skill of a curious mind. Instead of feeling like you have to defend yourself against the unknown, learning and using these skills can open up a whole new world of opportunity.

But sometimes, it's not as simple as deciding to embrace the unknown. Yes, choosing to change is a great start, but after that, we must be willing to fail forward to fill the gaps in our knowledge. The whole process requires intentional endurance, and if you're still in the space of healing your sense of self, you may not have the energy to embrace the unknown at this time. If this is you, keep reading. I'll be sharing more details on how to claim your sense of self in future chapters.

There's no two ways about it: a decision to change our lives is a layered experience of evolution. When you decide to change something, you must also evolve your thoughts and feelings, habits, and personality to meet the new reality. For example, leaving a job for a better one means learning the skills that come with the new position. You also have to see yourself as a person worthy of the promotion.

We can't decide to change, make the change, and not grow. In fact, we **have to** grow. If we are unable or unwilling to change, we will inevitably return to similar jobs, relationships, and circumstances we want to leave behind. Because we are influential creators of our reality, wherever we go, we create a reflection of who we are at that time. Thus, if we don't change, our lives can become Groundhog Day.

To create something different, we must be different. Changing the outer world requires a journey of evolution into our innermost thoughts and feelings. Similarly, a change in the inner world will reflect on our behavior in the outside world. Have you ever noticed how much easier it is to be disciplined about your success habits when you feel good about yourself? When you feel worthy of reaching your goals, it's easy to carry out the everyday activities required to get there.

So, if we want to improve something, we must learn to visit the discomfort of the unknown within ourselves and the world. Am I suggesting taking significant financial or practical risks in the name of your personal evolution? Of course not. I encourage you to make small, positive changes to learn how to get comfortable with the discomfort of change.

Challenging yourself to change in small, positive ways grows your personal evolution muscle. Even if small, frequent repetitions strengthen your capacity to deal with the unknown. This discomfort practice also prepares you for any big and unexpected things that are inevitable. Dealing with breakups, losing a job, or the challenges of parenting will be more productive experiences for you when you are able to embrace the unknown.

It was precisely this discomfort practice that made me feel comfortable about my decision to move to Ireland. There were so many instances where I could have backed off from leaving. Moving to a new job, living with strangers, and communicating in a language that was not my own was all very stressful. And get this. Back then, I did all the correspondence for my employment via letters. Actual. Written. Letters. Let that sink in. When I was twenty, I moved to a new country, knowing no one in person, and all the details were planned out and communicated using old-school correspondence.

This correspondence process took a lot of time and patience and is the perfect metaphor for what change looks like. Change is messy and unpredictable. Correspondence via letters showed me that so much could go wrong, and I had to learn to be okay regardless. One of the letters could have gotten lost in the mail, and I'd never get there. Or perhaps they withdrew the job offer, and when I turned up at the airport, no one was there to pick me up. If I wanted to become a wanderer, I had to decide that I would be fine no matter what happened with this job or my move to Ireland.

Over a decade later, when I moved to Australia to pursue my dream relationship with my partner, Peter, I took the same approach. I felt lucky to have stretched myself and strengthened my comfort zone throughout the years, including my move to Ireland. When I moved to Australia, literally to the other side of the world, I knew I would be fine no matter what.

Because I had adopted a habit of challenging myself to grow every year, I had become comfortable adjusting plans and making good decisions on the fly. If the relationship didn't work out, I would be okay. Regardless of the minor inconveniences that life and a new culture would bring my way, I knew that if I stayed curious about my change, everything would work out just fine.

Having lived in four countries, three of them for a decade or more, I see myself as a global citizen. While I make sure to honor the laws of different territories, I no longer think about the world as countries and borders. I don't see the countries as "us" and "them," and I don't subscribe to any country being "the greatest country in the world." Traveling globally and living my expat life has shown me the intricate ways that each country conducts itself. I have experienced enough to know that every country has its strengths and challenges.

I've also seen each country and its population undergo shared challenges. Remember, the process of maturation is cyclical in nature. Thus, every person and each population is deemed to experience the cycle of healing, building, thriving, destruction, and healing again.

I've realized that borders don't make us better or worse, but that all humans are fundamentally the same, just with different habits and traditions. While our appearance and cultural ideology differ, my travels have taught me that we all have precisely the same drives and issues, just to different degrees.

Every human thinks, feels, senses, and intuits. Every person has instincts, experiences, and conditioning. All people love in their own way, heal in their own way, and develop in their own way throughout their lives. The same is true for countries and populations.

Despite my personal traumatizing experiences, I view humankind as a big ocean full of treasures. It took me years to heal the past trauma and trust people, but when I did, my whole outlook on humanity changed. My work also affords me an inside track for insight. I have the opportunity to discover greatness hidden within my students' challenges every single day. Taking them deep diving for their inner treasures is thrilling. But there's nothing quite like helping them find their first pearl of inner wisdom and self-love. Every dive matters, every oyster is a new possibility, and every pearl is unique and beautiful.

My travels have been an excellent foundation for a basic understanding of the similarities and differences in humans. Having the great fortune of working with students from every continent except Antarctica keeps my life exciting. I love learning about cultural differences, and witnessing and understanding the uniqueness of people everywhere. This work leaves me feeling blessed and mentally awakened every single day.

My life has been so enriched by travel that I encourage everyone to spend at least six months living abroad if they can. The opportunities to heal, grow, and prosper are endless when we realize that our country of origin is not necessarily the ultimate expression of who we are as individuals. Simultaneously, travel can deepen our connection to our land of birth and can teach us a profound sense of gratitude for the culture we came from.

When you live abroad and work globally, you don't have the luxury of remaining ignorant about yourself or others around you. If you want to, you can learn to understand and find harmony with yourself and people of varying backgrounds and places of origin.

Being a wanderer gives you the kind of wisdom you cannot learn from a book or television. It's a lived experience that arises organically from every life situation. Thinking and imagining differ from doing. Moving to live abroad or even the next town over can give you a new perspective on yourself and life.

When you travel outside what you have accepted as "the norm," you challenge yourself to grow. This growth requires you to befriend and support yourself. You can let go of the parts of yourself you didn't choose and don't want to keep. You must show yourself patience and kindness as you learn to adapt to the new you.

You get to write the book of your life with the ending you prefer. No one else should have the power to decide who you are and who you are becoming. If you remove yourself from the known, you can discover the hidden treasures within you. The unknown world unveils the unknown gold that lies within you. Setting down the weight of others' opinions and your past conditioning helps you share your inner riches with the world.

So, who are you without your old baggage? Are you ready to dive into the unknown, embrace change, and find the treasures hidden deep within you?

Chapter 8

MANAGING EXPECTATIONS

"Change is inevitable. Growth is optional."
- JOHN C. MAXWELL

MANY OF US ARE DRIVEN to change because we want something better. A better home, a better relationship, a better environment, or a more suitable culture are all valid reasons for change. It feels so good to let go of the past bindings and step into a more bright, loving, and exciting future.

When we imagine the growth in our lives, we often focus on the perfection of the picture. How amazing would it feel to only have good times and feel loved and appreciated in life? Think about the last time you received unconditional love, or was told you did a good job. If you haven't experienced it, imagine how it would feel! Wouldn't it be nice if all we received were glowing compliments and open adoration from the world and the people around us?

It would be wonderful to keep diving deep into the ocean of our lives, knowing that any oyster you open, there would be the most magnificent pearl staring back at you. That. Would. Be. Awesome. Also, it would be a fantasy. Not every oyster carries a pearl.

To create a pearl, a grain of sand or other foreign substance must enter the oyster. The process of irritation and the oyster's attempts to heal the irritation end up creating a pearl. If we as humans want to create something similarly magnificent in our lives and our relationships, we can do it by adjusting our perception. Maybe all negative occurrences are not a bad thing. What if, like the oyster, we can take a proverbial blister in our lives and turn it into something valuable?

Not all forces outside our control are sinister, even if they may feel threatening. Circumstances we don't control may feel bad because it is us who have to be flexible. Essentially, we may feel threatened by what we don't command. But if we consciously stop labeling all unpredictability as unfavorable and choose to engage fully in the situation, we may discover many opportunities for delight and growth.

Growth and personal evolution are a tapestry of joyous and painful situations intertwined. We both bask in the glory of our inner light and are subject to life's negative feedback. To grow, we need safe spaces to navigate this dichotomy. Effectively, we need a shell to keep us safe while the frictions of the world force us to grow. Thus, a pearl is a perfect metaphor for personal evolution. It begins from external irritation and develops in the safety of the shell: the safe spaces we create.

There is simply no escaping it: if we want to make pearls from the negative experiences of our lives, we need pain, protection, and time to heal. We also must learn how to take action and to fail. To get a complete necklace of pearls, we may have to dive hundreds of times into life's challenging circumstances and our most painful memories. But a decision to dive is not enough. To set yourself up for success, you must also practice, fail, learn, and then practice some more. If you are a practiced diver, you will discover your life's treasures faster and with more ease. If you lack experience, be patient and ask for help from a more skilled diver. An experienced mentor will encourage and challenge you to grow.

When we decide to change on our own terms, - for example when we leave a relationship - the initial sense of freedom may feel intoxicating: we see positivity and opportunity everywhere. But after a while, the magic wears off. Such is the cyclical nature of human integration. Feeling free and powerful is just a plateau we reach before continuing our journey of personal evolution through a new flavor of discomfort. The initial high of a decision to change wears off and is replaced by hard work. Step by step, we must build an intentional new reality and learn to enjoy the challenges of growth. If we're not prepared to roll up our sleeves and get to work, the change we initiate begins to feel a lot like a burden. The inspiration to change is not enough, and relying on it alone can turn our vision into a trap.

Relationships are such a great example. If we simply move from one relationship to another without integrating our learnings, we jump from one honeymoon phase to another. We get so used to feeling elated by the new excitement and possibilities that we expect it to last forever. Once the novelty of newness wears off, you realize that happiness requires work, and that you were relying on feel-good hormones alone to keep your relationship on track.

When you're in love, you feel powerful and happy. But when the feel-good hormones stop flowing, you realize that - as an individual - you are not more empowered or happy. If you have used the new relationship as a distraction from your unhealed trauma, the realization that little has changed can lead to one of two outcomes:

1. Depression, because failing to hold on to the good feelings leads you to believe that something is fundamentally wrong with you or
2. Addiction because you want the good feelings back and will do anything to scratch that itch. That could even mean stepping outside your relationship for intimacy or

breaking up with your partner to move on to another honeymoon phase with someone else.

Getting addicted to positive feelings alone is a handbrake that stops us from having real interactions, authentic connections, and a happy life journey. Instead of demanding that the honeymoon phase with others lasts forever, we must realize that deep intimacy comes only after you've worked through significant struggles together. That means continuing to grow, even when everything isn't going well.

Knowing this could have saved many careers and relationships. Having realistic expectations would have smoothed out many potholes of life changes. The Hollywood love stories and old-school rom-coms are enjoyable but set an unrealistic standard. Lasting deep and authentic love requires struggle, growth, realism, and adjusted expectations. The same goes for our work and other major life decisions.

Having realistic expectations about your life and curiosity about life's unknowns can help stabilize you as you grow and evolve. You can enjoy the honeymoon period of a new relationship and still be practical about what does and does not work for you. Managing your expectations about life, work, and love might mean losing some external validation, but it is worth it.

You see, relying solely on external validation is a trap. The cocktail of validating feel-good hormones enters our bloodstream as drugs, and we fool ourselves into thinking that we see everything clearly. Too many politicians promise to solve our problems, and we trust them. They may tell you what you want to hear, but unless you keep them accountable for their promises, they can forget all about the people that got them elected! Have you ever voted for someone or entered a personal or business relationship and, after a year, realized the person was not who you thought they were? I sure have. To avoid this rude awakening, enjoy the validation, but don't forget to empower yourself by growing with life's challenges.

By not relying upon others to fix your problems and by embracing life's difficulties, you stay on track with your authentic growth. By understanding that life, love, and purpose are supposed to be both joyous and challenging, you can stay fully present with what you are creating. With authenticity and presence comes real positive change, genuine love, and the capacity to let others accept and embrace you just as you are.

When we manage our expectations, we can visualize success and stay grounded and productive at the same time. We learn to manage our expectations when we commit to inspired action instead of relying on wishful thinking. When we stop being overly critical or harsh with ourselves, we can find an opening to healthy relationships with ourselves, other people, and the entire world.

When we feel balanced and open, we realize that we are both amazing and unsavory. Our souls have the capacity to be both beautiful and ugly, and the same is true for everyone on this planet. We all struggle with the balance of grace and tactlessness, just to different degrees and in different situations. When we feel balanced and open, we can accept that we are only human, both the master and the beginner in our lives. We begin to extend compassion toward ourselves and others, and we start to see more commonalities than differences in one another.

If we rely on appearing perfect to feel good about ourselves, it's just a matter of time before we fall from grace. Humility is power. When we surrender our toxic ego and embrace who we are wholly, we can receive the world's feedback without getting upset. When we manage our expectations, we can take the reflections of the world seriously without taking them personally. That is when we stop fearing the unknown and entrust ourselves to the flow of life.

Chapter 9

THE FLOW OF LIFE

"Those who flow like life flows,
know they need no other force."

- LAO TZU

BEING IN THE PUBLIC EYE for a long time, I have learned the power of pause. For me, the pause has been the most potent tool when facing unsavory feedback and judgment about who I am or what I do. Being judged - especially for who you are - can be one of the most triggering experiences of your life. It's particularly marginalizing if you are criticized for something you had no power over. Taking shots at someone because of their color, gender, orientation, or socio-economic background is cheap. As you can see, I, too, can be judgy. But there's a difference between being judgemental and using judgment.

Being biased is like having an opinion. Everyone has one. You don't have to exercise critical thinking to have an opinion. You can simply say what's on your mind or how you feel. But using judgment is different. In order to use judgment, you have to be able to see your argument in the context of your values and personal experiences. And if you can take it a step further, you can study your judgment in the context of others' realities, too. It takes discipline to not become complacent or reactive in a world that seems to be full of judgment.

I work hard to stay vigorous when receiving judgment, too. When I get told that I'm too serious or that my work is too complicated, I pause. I want to take a moment to center myself on who I really am before responding. If I react and start appointing emotion to the feedback prematurely, I will likely miss out on an opportunity to grow.

You see, I don't want to reject an observation about me just because I'm having an emotional reaction to it. I want to know if, in fact, the observation has some merit and value to it. I press pause before responding because I want to work with the premise that others' observations about me are just feedback. I don't have to accept it if it feels wrong or irrelevant. If, after the pause, I feel compelled to respond to the feedback, I will take time to be thoughtful about it. If not, I will simply move on with my life. I don't believe that any feedback I receive makes me, you, or anyone else good or bad. It merely reflects our perspective at the time and how we are navigating through life as individuals.

If I buy into thinking that what I perceive to be negative feedback is only "bad," I end up deceiving myself. Rejecting what I perceive to be negative stops me from evolving, and sets me up to pretend like I'm perfect. There's nothing wrong with working to improve myself, but pretending to be perfect is a fool's errand. Perfection is an expectation which I can't possibly live up to. This drive for perfection will stop me from living my life fully. Perfection makes me too careful; I stop being a beginner. When I stop learning new things, it's just a matter of time before the world evolves beyond me, and I'm left in the dust defending my outdated opinions.

Similarly, when we attach to positive feedback, we tell ourselves lies that eventually catch up with us. If we inflate our sense of self and think that life always bends to our will, it's just a matter of time before we face a rude awakening. People with this kind of grandiose self-narrative keep pushing the boundaries to see how far they can take it. They are lulling themselves into a false sense of power that comes from every boundary they break and get away with. Refusing to accept others' boundaries or to hear anything negative creates a bubble that will inevitably burst.

I've seen myself start on this path of pretending to be perfect, and I can tell you, it's not sustainable. I have taken on too much because my ego wanted to feel important and invincible. I worked myself into the ground so as not to appear weak or ineffective. When I showed up from a toxic ego, I attracted people around me who were fraudulent, if not dangerous. After a particularly grueling exchange with a stalker, I finally surrendered to setting boundaries with my toxic ego. Pretending to be perfect had been too costly. Receiving "negative" feedback about whom I had let into my orbit finally sinked in when people I trusted and respected confronted me. Thank heavens for them and their harsh words. They stopped me going deeper into an abusive situation. Essentially, these loving people with their hard-to-hear feedback helped me change the course of my life for the better.

Ultimately, others' opinions are like boulders in the river of your life. Some offer you a safe space to rest, while others may bump or bruise you. If you've experienced abuse in your past, you know how hurtful some of these encounters can be. On the other hand, if you have ever experienced someone unconditionally holding space for the imperfect you, you know how nurturing it can be to rest on a boulder for a while.

Whether you are bruised or resting, you get to choose your boulders. Selecting what opinions you attach to, why, and for how long is totally up to you. When I started being more discerning about the boulders I focused on, my healing journey became easier to navigate. I would know which people would offer me a safe space, which ones would challenge me, and which ones would hold me accountable. My inner circle gave me a safe space to not be perfect. Thoughtfully facing my past bad decisions challenged me to grow, and my continuing work held me accountable going forward.

Deliberately choosing each boulder in this way invited me to grow beyond my past pain. I let go of the old story of being a victim and stopped giving my power away to my toxic ego, its desires, and others who would feed it. It took me a while to stop taking others' opinions to heart, but once I healed enough to realize that I was a sovereign being, I stopped resisting others' views and perceptions. This process taught me how to stop defending myself in the face of others' views because I realized that they were simply that: Opinions. They were just boulders I could choose to rest on, or use to challenge me. Pivoting my focus this way taught me that no matter what was going on in my life, I had the power to choose.

Even in my darkest moments, I have realized that I can turn my life around in a matter of minutes by simply exercising my power to choose. What do I want to focus on? What opinions do I want to release, and what do I want to respond to? Having the capacity to flip the narrative in this way gives me flexibility. It helps me to stay true to myself as I discover my pathway back to the magical flow of life.

Chapter 10

ARE YOU A PATHFINDER?

"Being a pathfinder is to be willing
to risk failure and still go on."

- GAIL SHEEHY

OUR CURRENT WORLD OF PERFECTIONISM, shame, and guilt
conditions most people to see themselves as failures and,
subsequently, as victims of circumstance. While some find my
outlook on personal ownership threatening or even misguided,
those who embrace it find it refreshingly empowering. Some hear
me say that you can continue to be a victim or become a pathfinder
to a more whole you and think, "Yeah, but you don't know how
hard my life is," or "It's easy for you to say because you've never
been hurt as I have."

Unless I have had a one-on-one conversation about their
circumstances, these people are right! I don't know. What I do
know is that I have experienced this perspective shift in myself
and supported thousands of others while they, too, have healed
themselves. I have seen people come from some of the most
horrifically torturous spaces and, over time, let go of the familiar
and comforting mantle of "a victim."

Before you think I'm judging people for not making the shift,
please let me put your mind at ease. I believe in the full agency

in people. In my mind, I, you, and everyone else have the right and power to live our lives exactly how is right for us. I'm talking about choosing the roles we want to express and master in our heart of hearts. The choice of seeing yourself as a victim or a Pathfinder is entirely yours, and it's also good to remember that victims rarely turn into Pathfinders overnight. It's a process that I want to discuss because I want to remind you of the power you have within yourself. **You**, not me, have the sovereignty to choose whatever is right for you!

When I talk about being invested in being a victim, I talk about the life we have built around the trauma we experienced at some point. It's usually a life of protection to keep us safe from ever being hurt again. If this is the case for you, I see you, and I respect you. Sometimes, we don't even remember who we were beyond the trauma persona, and to open that particular box can be scary or even, in some cases, too much for us to handle. If this is your current experience, I hear you. I have been there myself and understand firsthand what it's like.

When people, in all earnestness, ask me: "Is it possible to become a Pathfinder even though I have experienced all this trauma?" Based on what I have lived and seen with my students, my answer is a resounding "Yes." It's rarely an immediate shift, but it is possible for most of us. I have seen thousands of people become Pathfinders despite and even **because of** their past painful experiences.

This is not to encourage thoughtless spiritual bypasses. Thinking that this change is simple or that trauma only strengthens us is ignorant. Certainly, many personal development "gurus" sell their products or services under the guise of this false premise: "5 easy steps of healing your inner child", and so on. Make no mistake: if you have experienced severe trauma, becoming a Pathfinder is not simply a question of deciding to follow "5 easy steps". While reading an article that oversimplifies your experience can be helpful in forming a big picture of your current challenges, it's rarely enough to help you heal. Moving from victimhood to becoming a Pathfinder requires both a decision and deep work that is worth doing.

But it's not all bad news. Where you are right now is the perfect place to start. Many feel too deeply rooted in the darkness to realize that past trauma can serve as a lantern for them. The light of our past pain can help illuminate a path to a meaningful life. So not only is trauma *not stopping you* from finding your way in life, but it may even *help you* identify it faster when you work *with it*.

A person who has suffered severe childhood trauma is more likely to know what they don't want. This can be half the battle. By exploring their dislikes and past pain, they become clear on what they *do* want, even if they struggle to verbalize it at first. Learning to share our likes and dislikes may also connect us to others who can relate to our experiences on a profound level. This is why many past victims have gone from healing their own struggles to helping others overcome theirs. While not all trauma survivors become mentors or therapists, they tend to find ways to live intentionally and contribute to the world in a meaningful way.

So, wherever you find yourself right now, it's ok. The family you come from and how you are built and conditioned is not nearly as important as betting on yourself. A great way to start is getting to know your likes and dislikes. Being willing to look for any patterns that arise from your authentic preferences can help you discover a golden thread of insight within you. If you keep following this golden thread of insight faithfully, you stay on track while transcending most familial conditioning you have experienced. That golden thread of sovereignty is the key to unveiling the genius that lives within you.

I also encourage you not to hide your inner genius. Having the courage to fully share yourself with safe others can help you immensely. Often, if we keep our hearts open, we receive the exact message from others we most need to hear. In fact, I have yet to meet a person who has been able to heal and master their life without input from trusted others. Asking for help is a sign of strength. No matter how entangled the golden thread of your sovereignty has become because of pain and trauma, with proper support - and continuing self-care - you can untangle it, follow it, and uncover the genius at the other end.

There's another profound benefit to sharing your preferences with others. When others become aware of your likes and dislikes, they are better able to interact with you in a meaningful way. Many trauma survivors don't like shallow conversations. We complain when others want to talk about weather and wish they would share something real instead. But we rarely take the steps to make this happen. We either refuse to make small talk, thus closing potential for deep connections down before they can be built, or we become emotionally slutty, oversharing details from our lives. The latter way of being usually either scares people away or attracts those who look to capitalize on our personal details when the opportunity arises.

Knowing who to trust is as simple as observing how others treat us when our needs are an inconvenience for them. Those who do what they can for us even when there's nothing in it for them is a good place to start. Sharing your likes and dislikes with these people **mindfully** and **gradually** is a powerful way to discover, build, and fortify meaningful human connections.

Alongside healing and cultivating supportive relationships, becoming a Pathfinder is a beautiful learning experience. Firstly, when you become a Pathfinder, **your capacity to notice and seize growth opportunities accelerates**. When you become intentionally curious, you begin to recognize the opportunities to grow through a repertoire of feelings. The most common emotions we feel as Pathfinders are confusion, curiosity, and delightful surprise. When you observe a situation and wonder how it unfolded, you are in a space of growth.

Secondly, **your attitude toward learning new skills becomes more curious.** How do you feel when the world shows you that you are incompetent in utilizing a specific skill? A victim will go down a rabbit hole of self-pity and defensiveness. The victim denies themselves an opportunity to learn, and they over-rely on the skills they have already acquired. When you're a victim and only have a hammer, every screw looks like a nail. The Pathfinder, on the other hand, asks questions. They see their incompetence as a challenge to grow and acquire new tools. Sure, initially, they may struggle using a screwdriver, but they understand that taking the time to learn a new skill will end up taking much less time in the long run.

What will you do when the world tells you something that does not fit your current picture of yourself? Do you double down and take a defensive stance, fearing losing yourself to the world? Or do you learn to take the journey of the Pathfinder by asking questions and discovering a lens more expansive than your old one? The choice is yours. Don't let your already invested time and resources talk you into staying a victim. When you become a Pathfinder, you will get back the money and time you have already invested in your pain, and much, much more.

Once you have decided to pursue your life as a Pathfinder and established your physical, practical, and psycho-emotional self-care, you begin to see new opportunities everywhere. Remember, this journey is not black and white. You don't simply decide and *poof* now you have become a Pathfinder for life.

There are times when you will doubt if you can do this. There will be times when you tell yourself that it's too hard. In these moments, I encourage you to remember that you are human and that adjusting to a new role or outlook takes time. Becoming a Pathfinder of healing and growth is a dance of both remembering your inner brilliance and expecting to fail forward. There is no "perfect score" you can get in personal evolution.

It can be hard to let go of the victim's persona if you have experienced severe abuse. I know this from personal experience. It is hard for the victim to see themselves as the genius they actually are beneath the protective story of their past pain. It's much easier to not rock the boat and ignore the golden thread. It took me a long time to admit that I, too, was more than a victim. It took me a long time to accept that I had something significant to share. To discover the genius within me, I had to prioritize my golden thread, become curious about myself and my experience. I had to stop seeing myself as a two-dimensional character in someone else's story.

Recognizing my inner genius and following the golden thread of "me" taught me new skills. Allowing myself to fail forward made my life more manageable, because I no longer wasted time and resources in appearing to be perfect. When I stopped demanding perfection from myself and others, and took on the role of a beginner and a learner, I became a Pathfinder. Every day became a new opportunity for more healing and self-mastery.

There is so much we can learn from taking on the challenges life gives us every day. Being earnestly inquisitive will help us build better relationships at home and work. We can also meld into new communities and societies more easily. Once we decide to become a beginner again, we can start asking connection-oriented questions, such as:

1. How do others see this issue?
2. What are others' thoughts on this topic?
3. What experience do others have with this activity?
4. What might others think the solution is?

Becoming inquisitive is hard. You are changing your narrative from "I know" to "What don't I know." This change in and of itself can feel threatening because it's questioning everything you think is true. You may feel nervous the first time you ask these questions, even as an internal inquiry. The stakes are even higher when you ask these questions in conversations with others. I remember fearing that people would label me stupid if I asked questions.

Back then, I was under the false impression that asking questions was a sign of weakness. I have learned since then that **not asking questions** is a sign of insecurity.

A secure mind is open. The most intelligent, mature, and confident people ask questions because they would rather learn and have positive exchanges than talk all the time and hear their own thoughts reflected in an echo chamber.

Pathfinders dare ask questions because others' answers cannot sabotage their sense of self. They know in their bones that others' views are just opinions they can take on board or not. Pathfinders have concluded that all humans share the same thoughts, fears, and hopes, only in different forms and order of priorities. They have realized that we all have different degrees of the same challenges. By stripping away cultural, religious, political, racial, gender, and other roles, Pathfinders encourage themselves and others to show up and interact authentically - simply as human beings.

Asking thoughtful questions allows Pathfinders to discover who they are to other people. Are they neighbors, lovers, friends, or colleagues? Are they enemies, frenemies, irritants, or catalysts for growth? Is the other person a safe space, a negative interaction to be had, or an opportunity to grow?

Additionally, Pathfinders don't compare or compete. They see others' achievements as an inspiration to develop themselves further and work to discover solutions that serve them and those they are responsible for.

Do you see yourself as a Pathfinder? Do some of what I have outlined here speak to you? Maybe all of it? Perhaps you're not sure. If you have any confusion, don't worry. I, too, had to discover my inner Pathfinder through living life and working with a mentor. My life as a Pathfinder has not been just "an interesting experience" for me. It has become a lifestyle and profound work worth doing.

Chapter 11

WORK WORTH DOING

"Before enlightenment, chop
wood, carry water.
After enlightenment, chop
wood, carry water."

- ZEN SAYING

FOR THE LONGEST TIME, I have been fascinated by work, jobs, careers, and vocations. I've been working on defining the differences and the importance of each of them.

For me, work is a description of the activity that I undertake to complete any given task. A job is a role I take on to complete the work that needs to be done. My career is a collection of jobs I have taken on. My vocation is the driving force behind my career. For me, vocation is not a job, nor is it work. Vocation is a conviction that keeps me on track with a meaningful and happy life.

According to the Gallup 2014 poll, fifty-five percent of workers in the United States get a sense of identity from their jobs. This statistic is interesting because it suggests that nearly half of the measured workforce does not receive a sense of identity from their work roles.

It made me wonder if forty-five percent of the working population is psychologically healthy or simply disengaged from their jobs. About half of the people I've spoken with are highly satisfied with their work but identify themselves primarily through their families and hobbies. Is the other half focused on hump days and Fridays instead of enjoying their work?

This two-dimensional way of thinking - that you either love or hate your job - started me on another track of thought. Surely, we don't simply fall into these two categories. There has to be more to work, jobs, careers, and vocations than merely being content or discontent with it. So, I took a moment and started rolling back the work reel of my life, looking for patterns. I discovered that I had never related to work in this binary way. Instead, I realized that neither work nor my personal life outside work had ever defined me as a person.

Many find this statement odd or even off-putting. So many of us define who we are by our jobs, cars, hobbies, families, and education. However, I'm different. Instead of looking for who I am in what I do, I define myself by how authentically I show up and how in alignment with my dream life I am in my everyday interactions.

For me, work has always been a playground and an opportunity to learn, grow, and create something meaningful in life. Every job has taught me something precious. As a cleaning lady in a candy factory, I learned the importance of confidentiality. When you take out someone's trash, you realize who they are and how they conduct themselves. In my role of cleaning stables in a riding school, I learned how to support students and make their horsemanship experience more pleasurable and fun.

I could have simply gone to work, done what the job description mandated, and gone home. But honestly, that would have felt inauthentic. My work had to satisfy my curiosity for life. As a curious person, I wanted to know how my work positively or negatively impacted the end result and what I could do to increase the level of the beneficial effect. I now know that this proactive stance in looking for solutions is why I kept getting promoted into leadership positions in most jobs.

Alongside traveling the world and embracing everything it offered, I have never shied away from work and the opportunities it brought to develop myself. Since I finished school, I have not spent one day without a job. This is not to say that I judge others on their authentic path or criticize those who cannot work. It's simply a reflection of my insatiable yearning for knowledge and play.

Many mistakenly believe they must work in their "own" industry to learn something of value. In my experience, this is not true. Of course, everyone deserves to pursue their dream job! But life has taught me that all work, every job, and every career can be life-changing.

Many project a false sense of security to the exact "right" role or position. They project outward that their lives will magically be better if they only have the "right job." While your work life may become more pleasurable, your experience will not automatically become smooth sailing just because you have a job you identify with.

The real sense of security in life comes from knowing that the power of direction is within you, not in your job or a boss. Something magical happens when you realize your inner power and how to engage with it through any work: life starts flowing toward your preferred job or role.

In the meantime, I recommend you learn everything you can from your current job: your personal power, enjoyment of life, productivity, loving boundaries - and, of course, the technical know-how you'll pick up on the way.

My personal experience has taught me that you can learn new skills and actualize "the essence of you" in any available job. Whether you are a prestigious business leader, innovator, first responder, or window washer, you are still *the incredible you!*

Instead of relying on the right job or position for a sense of status or security in life, your attitude decides your fate. A "rolling up your sleeves" stance equals security. Any job can change your life if you are willing to learn and work smart.

People who over-identify with their work tend to overlook the fact that every job comes with transferable skills. Instead of focusing on not having your dream career, I encourage you to focus on learning a skill you can take with you when the right opportunity comes along.

If I couldn't get a job in my preferred profession, I would apply for those I most liked from what was available. Maybe your current job is not perfect, but that doesn't mean you can't work toward your "perfect" job. Perhaps your career has taken an unexpected turn, but it's simply a side-step to gain your balance and surge forward again.

A long-time friend and confidant of mine - let's call him Tom, as he is a very private person - is an inspiring example of someone who masterfully transfers skills from one job and career to another. His original work was as a horse veterinarian, after which he went into business and then back into the veterinary field, but now in a corporate capacity. Tom is the embodiment of transferable skills. I would even say he is a genius in that way. He continues to rise to opportunities. As a result, more opportunities follow.

Thank heavens, I learned that every job matters. Had I thought that being a cleaning lady was beneath me, I would have missed out on the transferable skills I learned. Discretion, quiet service, and genuine support of others are just some of the lessons I took with me. To this day, I am utilizing these skills in my business and while working with my students. I am grateful for being allowed to hold that job, if even for less than a year.

[A note from the authors: Lisa and I want to thank all cleaning professionals worldwide! Every time we see one of these tireless professionals at work, we take a moment to thank them. Shopping centers, houses, factories, airports - wherever we travel, we want to thank you. We love and respect you. Thank you for your work. You are amazing.]

My work, regardless of the genre, has taught me life skills, communication skills, skills for relating to others, and skills of accountability and humility. When I combined these transferable skills with gratitude, I was presented with more opportunities than I could manage.

Chapter 12

COMMIT TO SHOWING UP

"Being perfect is not nearly as
important as showing up."

- MERJA SUMILOFF

Since my days of employment, I have built several six-figure-a-year businesses from the ground up with no seed money. Many have asked me how I was able to generate the results and repeat them after my initial success. I put my hits down to four things:

- A vision that fills my heart
- Transferable skills
- Being a beginner, and
- Committing to showing up as the best version of myself.

Something magical happens when we align ourselves with our vision. It's like the Universe says: "Thank you for finally being clear about what you want!" By owning my vision, I stepped into a paradigm that both carries me and challenges me to grow. When I stop demanding perfection from myself and cease trying to control my environment, my eyes relax, and my perception becomes wider. By switching from a direct-line way of thinking to a bigger picture, I begin to see the transferable skills in the periphery of my field of focus.

Most weeks, something happens in business that challenges me to grow. I look at the situation from different angles and see what the suitable solution could be. If there's no obvious fix to the problem, instead of getting stressed, I relax into my peripheral field of vision to look for a less conscious solution over there. I ask myself: "In what other area of my life have I overcome this same situation before?" More often than not, I *seem* to generate a solution to a business challenge from "thin air."

But of course, these solutions don't come from thin air. They come from showing up, focusing, and tapping into my transferable skills. When I enter this space of flow, I can simply stay present with what life brings me and enjoy the journey. I am dynamic, resilient, and enthusiastic at work because I want to be. I want to make the most of my work so that I can continue to master my craft. Do I always feel this way? Oh no!

There are days when I feel flat or even depressed instead of dynamic. On those days, *I make a commitment to myself to show up and do my best.* There are also times when I am not resilient. Sometimes I'm crumbling under the unimaginable weight of responsibility and heartbreak. On those days, *I remind myself that I only have to take one step at a time.* Instead of thinking about how I have to perform for the rest of my life, I only focus on the next ten minutes.

And boy, are there times when I can't muster enthusiasm for my work. When I'm sick or treated poorly by a client or a colleague, I simply have no energy to be enthusiastic. On those days, *I'm honest about what is going on with me without making others responsible for how I'm feeling.* Honesty, authenticity, and good old-fashioned grit have made me a popular employee in the past and a success in business over the last couple of decades. I know that by committing to showing up and doing my best, it's just a matter of time before I succeed.

But mastering my craft does not mean that I strive for perfection. Perfection does not bring happiness or peace. The process of self-discovery does. Focusing on the journey and not the destination gives us a sense of accomplishment and self-acceptance on the way. The power of self-actualization through work is often understated. Many like me, who come from humble beginnings, agree that by working their way up in the world, they have discovered themselves in a profound way and learned to respect themselves in the process. It wasn't the job that gave us our sense of identity. It was us doing the job in a proactive, discovery-oriented way.

We can mistakenly believe that to become who we really are, we must take time off to sit on the top of a mountain for a month or that we must be privileged. It is a common belief that we must be more, do more, and be outwardly prosperous to become our true selves fully. This is not true.

Yes, I agree that every person should be paid a living wage and that a solid social security structure should be in place to ensure that no citizen is left behind. And just to be clear, money is a wonderful thing to have! But wealth does not automatically make us more integrated. Living in line with our internal values, thoughts, and feelings does. When we are clear and solid about who we are, we live from that place, and the need to make an impression disappears. We simply show up in meetings with others and the world as we are: imperfectly perfect.

Sure, money is nice to have. Of course, we need money to live in this modern world, but what if your actualized self had less to do with your paycheck and more to do with how you show up to work? Then who would you be? What if, instead of focusing on titles and the wage alone, you were to realize yourself and your full potential quietly? No fuss, no hype, just chopping wood and carrying water.

I have seen my students use this quiet focus to unlock healing and actualize their dream careers. I have also seen them heal relationships, set necessary boundaries, and even bring about great wealth by simply focusing on their own journey. When we integrate ourselves, we show up as the best version of ourselves and do our work from that space. When we operate from our best selves, we become more attractive to others and previously unseen opportunities.

Bringing your best self to any situation refers to your current best self. For some, that's making massive business deals every month; for others, it's honoring their grieving process or being able to take a shower when struggling with depression. Your best self right now is the best version of yourself you can muster. Do not compare your best self to that of someone else's. That, my friend, would be like comparing apples and oranges.

If you want to be vocationally satisfied, I challenge you to try this:

- Keep the vision of your dream job in mind and do your absolute best with every current task in front of you.
- Learn the skills you need to step into a role more aligned with your authentic self and repeat.
- On the days you struggle, be honest with yourself and others, own your challenge, and do your best. This approach enables you to live according to your intrinsic values as you fulfill your duties.

Remember, skills are transferable. Don't overlook a mundane task just because it seems meaningless to you. Discover **how** that task can help you with your next life stage.

So, now, my dear reader, I have three questions for you. I trust you to ask yourself these questions about the area of your life that you most identify with and want to transform. If it's your career, then that's great. If you want to empower yourself around relationships, then utilize them for that. Whatever area of life you focus on, ask yourself:

1. What skills have you learned from previous experiences to help you with your current pursuits?
2. What skills do you need to learn - right now - to have a better future?
3. Where can you learn those skills?

If this feels daunting, don't fret. For those of us who have experienced childhood abuse, aiming to make the most of our lives may feel impossible. Usually, when we feel overwhelmed, it's a sign that we are worried about failing. We either fear that we are not perfect, or we don't trust our sense of deservedness. That's when taking the attitude of "failing forward" comes in handy. Learn to slow down and redirect your attention. When you stop focusing on the perfection or the number of tasks, and instead begin *learning through the tasks*, you're set.

But for some of us, it's not that simple. We look at all that is possible, and are unable to commit to our goals and dreams, or even the process of learning through the tasks. We may not feel worthy of success. We may not believe that we deserve new opportunities. We may not realize that working *with* these feelings are the pathway to our inner power.

Chapter 13

ON THE BRINK OF POWER

"If it's important to YOU, it IS important."

- PETER HAGERTY

*A*T THIS STAGE, YOU MAY think: "That's great, Merja, but what about me? I don't feel like I have the right to my dreams. I don't believe that I am important. People around me are not supporting me. I can't put myself out there and self-advocate because people and situations have hurt me in the past. I don't trust people, I feel constantly criticized, and I can't relax." And to that, I say: "I hear you, and I see you."

For some of us, especially those who have experienced betrayal trauma, it's not as simple as having a vision or setting a goal and then going for it. For some of us, healing is a big part of the process of "getting out there" in the world, and living a happy and meaningful life. Knowing how hard healing can be makes me feel honored when others share their stories of trauma recovery with me.

I receive weekly messages and emails from those who want to find a way out of their dark forest of pain. I have helped thousands of people worldwide to take their past trauma and turn it into an origin story for a successful life.

These people were ready to change, let go of what had held them back, and take a chance on themselves. Yes, the painful past had disenchanted them, but they decided to reclaim their power because they realized they deserved to live a brighter, more loving, and more meaningful future.

If every one of these people wrote a memoir, my bookshelves would be full of stories of empowerment. You see, *you* get to write the ending to your story, no matter how arduous your journey has been to date and what adversities you have endured.

However, if you feel stuck, you're not alone. Some of us can get overwhelmed by our daunting past and repeatedly enter a spiral of disempowerment and depression. Some of us need a break from everything nightmarish because even thinking about the past can feel retraumatizing. And some of us feel totally alone with our pain, with no perceivable way out.

I see this kind of struggle and loneliness every day. I've certainly been there, and it's not all in the past. On my darkest days of painful losses or traumatic events, I still travel to the depths of my hopelessness and pain. **Thankfully, I now know that my pain is not all of who I am.** I have implemented strategies to work as life savers when I dive too deep and can't find my own way out.

Even when I'm scared, I have learned not to run from my pain. I've learned to respect my pain, even befriend it, so that together, we can understand the lessons that propel my life forward. I even take time to thank my past pain for giving me insight into how we, as humans, can profoundly and authentically relate to one another. Befriending and healing our pain and grief can become superpowers guiding us on our purposeful life journey. It's certainly what happened in my case.

Working with my painful past has put me on a track that helps others do the same. My healing journey taught me to embrace trauma-informed principles in everything I do. By befriending and developing a relationship with all parts of me, I discovered how to start making the most of my life. But it wasn't until I created a measurable system for mastering my life that I could begin to pass on the benefits of this work to others. Putting together a structure that speaks to every part of us ensures that no stone on our healing journey remains unturned. By sharing my structure through the Sumiloff Academy, I can continue to guide others through the darkest moments of their lives.

This structure birthed my healing, development, and life mastery curriculum. By showing my students how to befriend their pain while finding balance in the outside world, they can step into their own empowerment. They learn how to keep one eye on healing their past pain and the other on their desired life. By systematically breaching this gap, they overcome their painful past so that they are equipped to meet life's challenges head-on and go for whatever lights up their souls.

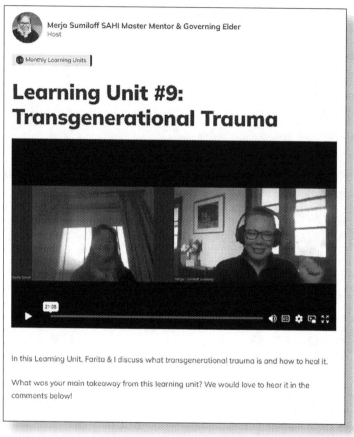

Merja Sumiloff SAHI Master Mentor & Governing Elder
Host

Monthly Learning Units

Learning Unit #9:
Transgenerational Trauma

In this Learning Unit, Farita & I discuss what transgenerational trauma is and how to heal it.

What was your main takeaway from this learning unit? We would love to hear it in the comments below!

The Sumiloff Online Academy helps its students heal, develop, and master their lives.

This apparent polarity of accepting our starting point and choosing to grow beyond it is the most fertile soil for our personal empowerment. Our students know that it's okay and normal to both be in pain and wanting to heal at the same time. Unfortunately, the common narrative is that you're either a victim or a powerhouse and that there's nothing in between. But that's not real life. I have yet to find a person who is only a victim or a superhero. We can be both, sometimes even at the same time. It is completely natural to be flawed and simultaneously have the yearning to level up your life.

As simple as it sounds, bridging the gap between where you are and where you want to be is not necessarily easy. It takes practice to stay open to past painful emotions while simultaneously challenging old perspectives and learning new skills. Teaching ourselves to navigate this new way of becoming requires two - what appear to be - opposite skills: holding space and setting boundaries.

Like many children, the safest I have ever felt in my life was when I was taken seriously, but also given caring and thoughtful bounds. Because receiving this kind of parenting was not consistent for me, I had to learn how to offer this space of security for myself. When I learned to hold space and set boundaries with myself, I was able to give myself a sense of security I needed to heal my childhood wounds. Did I always love this process? Heck no! But I have come to accept that some parts of me are mature enough to handle life, while others are not.

Much of the time, our trauma thrives in the less developed parts of us. This is where setting loving boundaries with those parts is essential. By guiding them with love, we can offer them safety as the more developed parts create a life that is compassionate, focused, and productive. But this doesn't mean that I abandon the less developed, less fluent, and traumatized parts of me. Through loving attention and boundaries, I, and we all, can create an internal safe space where our trauma can heal, we can develop, and mature into a purposeful creator of our desired life.

When loving and caring, the boundaries we give ourselves create a container for who we are, who we are becoming, and how to get there. I see loving boundaries as a support structure, not a way to control ourselves or others.

When we receive loving boundaries from others, we get to know them for exactly who they are.

When we accept loving boundaries from ourselves, life calms down and we get to know ourselves in a more deep and meaningful way.

For example, when my partner insists that I rest, it's because he is a kind and caring person who wants me to look after myself. When I set loving boundaries with myself by cutting down on caffeine, I make a statement that my long-term health is more important than giving in to a short-term fix. While small, these loving boundaries have the power to transform ourselves and our lives over time.

Boundaries with others help us show up as the best version of ourselves in our relationships. They stop us from oversharing or having unrealistic expectations of ourselves and others. Loving boundaries can also be a shorthand for communicating with those we love, especially in challenging situations. I remember when Peter and I had to evacuate from the 2019/2020 bushfires. The loving boundaries we had established with each other before the fires helped us through this devastating and potentially lethal experience. You can imagine how distressing the experience was and how two introverts could have had a hard time claiming the time to decompress amid it. Our pre-existing, loving boundaries had conditioned us to communicate our needs for alone time without hesitation.

To be truly empowered requires the skills of setting and accepting boundaries without casting derogatory meanings on them. Thinking that you are a terrible person for setting boundaries or that others are trying to hurt you by setting theirs may add another layer of complexity to your already challenging attempt to heal. If we can simply let go of the idea of boundaries being only negative, we have a higher probability of healing. The bottom line is that trying to heal our trauma without loving boundaries to contain it is nearly impossible. Without the support structure of loving boundaries, our trauma may run rampant poisoning areas of our lives that are important to us.

I've seen many traumatized people ruin their finances, relationships and health because they refuse to see boundaries as something positive or useful. Over time, and as the struggle escalates, they align themselves with their trauma, because they don't believe they deserve anything better. Soon after aligning themselves with their trauma, they begin to identify with it. It becomes a part of who they are, and as such, their reality.

They begin to prioritize their painful past over any current opportunities. Instead of relating to the present moment with an open mind, they see others' actions through the lens of a victim. They isolate themselves from the world that isn't treating them well. As their sense of loneliness grows, the light within them continues to die. Breaking this pattern and re-lighting our inner flame takes effort, support, and leaning into the structure of loving boundaries.

Sharing our stories of trauma with others can help us heal as we let go of the shame we have carried within us. But loving boundaries may be needed here too! There is a difference between focusing on and sharing our trauma with others so that we can process it, and strengthening our identification with trauma by roping others into our victim story. When we co-create with others from our vibe of trauma, we attract others into our struggle. This is how trauma-bonded relationships are born.

Are you finding yourself in a trauma-bonded relationship? Have you ever wished your trauma away, so that your circumstances would change? Have you ever thought that your life would have been so much better if only you had not been hurt in the past?

Before discovering that beneath my deepest wound is my greatest gift to the world, this was me. I was worried that I was damaged goods. My pre-healing self was concerned that I had wasted my life because of the burden of my childhood pain. But that wasn't to be the end of my story. By setting loving boundaries, and putting my trauma to work, I was able to heal and thrive.

If this speaks to you, please know that you are at the brink of your power. While initially painful, acknowledging that you are not happy or don't feel respected is a great place to start setting loving boundaries. Like our students at the Academy, I'd like to encourage you to accept your own significance, even when you're not perfect. You - even with trauma - matter. You - even with self-sabotaging patterns - deserve to heal and have a happy and meaningful life. You - at this exact moment - are at the brink of your personal power: you are about to start bridging the gap between who you are and who you want to be. And the first step to building that bridge is your awareness of the darkness you have been living in.

Part III

AMAZING GRACE

Chapter 14

VISITING THE DARKNESS

"Pain helps us grow if we respect,
listen to, and heal from it."

- MERJA SUMILOFF

MANY MISTAKENLY THINK THAT WE overcome our darkness by simply acknowledging it. It's like we believe that by accepting our pain, we have healed it. I don't think that's accurate. In my experience, doing the work to heal is much harder than simply admitting that we were hurt. Merely wandering into the darkness of our past is not enough; healing only happens when we begin to map out the darkness, befriend it, and learn to use it for our benefit.

Without creating healthy guardrails around the darkness in our lives, we can become trauma-focused or even obsessed. We may walk down the slippery paths of the dark forest just to see how far we can go. This is especially true if our trauma has been deeply lodged into our brain's memory center, the hippocampus. Our hippocampus is responsible for creating storylines for our lives and making sense of the past. If we can't set boundaries with ourselves and our thoughts, we can simply become lost in the dark forest of our past pain. In severe cases, we may need help from qualified mental health professionals to interrupt the trauma replay, and restructure the story of our lives.

While working with a professional is important, there are many skills we can utilize ourselves. Learning to set and maintain loving boundaries with our past pain, thoughts, and fears will serve us well when we decide to explore the darkness. These guardrails can help keep us safe as we journey into the dark forest, and they can also stop us from going too deep, too quickly. Setting loving boundaries with our thoughts can keep us psychologically safe as we navigate our recovery process. After all, we want to visit our trauma to befriend and harness it, not settle into the darkness permanently and watch the world go by.

What happens when we visit the guard-railed dark forest? As we consciously stay with our pain and grief, our eyes start getting used to the darkness. By acknowledging our pain, we learn to observe it and find balance in the uneven, unexplored landscape. We realize that much of our life has been built around our trauma and that we have a choice about keeping it as is, or slowly starting to change it. As we lovingly begin reordering the trauma beliefs that have created our current life, our brain begins to adjust to the new reality and world order. It is this sense of new, claimed sovereignty from our pain that begins to open our minds to the kind of life we *do* want to build.

The clearer we get, the more sure our stride becomes. With each balanced step, we decisively move into our *chosen* direction. It's like each step is an affirmation that our trauma is a separate entity from who we are (or want to be) and that we can start extending grace and compassion for the past, victimized version of ourselves. But remember to approach your pain with caution and care. If you force it, like a stray dog, your trauma may bite or scratch you. Don't rush through the darkness; befriending your trauma may take a while.

As you approach your pain slowly and with care, it begins to trust you. At this point, you can gently ask yourself: "Why am I here in the dark forest? What do I need to learn?". When you are no longer driven by the pain or the coping mechanisms you have adopted to survive, then, as if magically, the answers begin to flow. Your mind slows down to almost a space of tranquility as you realize the true purpose of your visit to the forest: to discover who you are without your pain. As Peter Hagerty says, "The dark night of the soul is an exploration of our true self through and beyond our pain."

This part is scary, especially if your hippocampus has been heavily invested in your coping mechanisms. You may realize you're in the wrong line of work or relationship or live in the wrong country. You may hit a point of confusion where you have no idea who you are anymore.

This is the time when most people bug out. The fear of uncertainty and potentially losing the life they have built drives them out of the dark forest. Although it seems they escaped the darkness, a heavy shadow of self-doubt follows them around. On some level, they know that if they had chosen to stay in the dark forest, they could have relaxed deeper into their pre-trauma identity and forged their past pain into a helpful tool for their future adventures.

Returning to our pre-trauma self brings about a life of infinite possibilities. By letting go of the trauma, we give ourselves *a certainty of choice*. Staying with the pain long enough to feel a new sense of freedom demolishes the urge to run from our pain again. Instead of giving into the knee-jerk reaction of changing careers, relationships, or countries, our newly-discovered, empowered self has the capacity to make the most of anything in life. It's incredible how often our jobs, people, and environments grow with us. When we feel powerful, we don't have to leave our lives behind just because we shed our toxic coping mechanisms.

Many call this part the ego death. I would not go that far. After all, a healthy ego is an essential drive for human survival and actualization. I call it an ego surrender. The part of ourselves that has tried to control everything and everyone around us is finally able to let go, relax, and transform.

After the moment of surrender, the ego can heal, discover its proper form, and become purposeful. Until the point of healing, our ego may have driven a hidden personal agenda stemming from our innermost insecurities. We all have them. But at this moment of ego surrender, many of my students have stopped navel-gazing and begun serving the greater good of their communities or the world. When our ego surrenders and heals, its drive has the power to change the world in unimaginable, positive ways.

As the ego surrenders, a period of grief follows. We enter a hippocampal review process that forces us to take time as we reorder our thoughts and rebuild our life's story reel. Almost everything we thought we knew has forever changed. It is a neurobiological necessity to reorder the brain before we can move on. It can be challenging, like learning to do things with your non-dominant hand. At first, new thoughts feel awkward, and imagining yourself as someone other than a victim can feel challenging. But I encourage you to trust the process.

As our thoughts reorder, an authentic version of ourselves emerges to challenge us. The challenge is self-prioritization. To heal fully, we must learn to become unwilling to compromise our core values or needs. Of course, we may have a hangover of past conditioning, but as we change, we are no longer driven by others' compromising wants and needs. Instead, we give ourselves the ultimate permission to live a life where, most of the time, our authentic needs and core values are being met.

If you're anything like me, you've realized that your toxic ego - unexpectedly - has also served you. By holding on to my past pain, my unhealthy ego has worked tirelessly to protect me against any future abuse. You can see why it would be hard for me to let go of something that has kept me safe for such a long time. Viewing the toxic ego this way, you can see how it has been the white knight in my story of survival.

Imagine my confusion when I was told by a mental health professional that to heal and become myself truly, I had to "kill" my protector, the white knight, my toxic ego. Thank heavens I didn't listen to him. Instead, I followed my intuition and asked the knight if he was willing to heal, transform, and integrate with me. I wanted him to become an ally and not fight to keep me trapped in my fears. He said "yes," and so a fundamental healing union was born. The scared little girl began to transform into the empowered woman I am today.

This union lit a flame within my soul that has illuminated my path in and out of the dark forest *at will*. Knowing that my old guardrails are still in place, I no longer have to be scared as I travel in, out, and through my past pain. Because of these rails and my inner alliance, I have never again felt unsafe, nor blinded by the darkness.

But many don't understand the inevitability of grief from the toxic ego's surrender. We mistakenly think healing is only a positive experience and should exclusively follow a predetermined upward trajectory. Entering grief, these projectors get confused and, in their disorientation, try to control the healing process. They mistakenly think something must be wrong with them because their healing journey was not all song and dance. They secretly shame themselves for not healing on schedule or in "the perfect way." If they only knew that healing is never perfect. While it's worth it, it's also messy and ugly and complicated.

If we judge our healing process prematurely and shame ourselves for not being perfect, we settle into what I call "the murky waters of self-oppression." Some find these waters soothing. At least if we judge, shame, blame, and oppress ourselves, no one else can beat us to the punch. The most challenging part of resting in these waters is that we halt the hippocampal review process. If we can stay away from the murky waters of self-oppression, we can continue to write a new ending to our story. Persecuting ourselves for not being perfect at healing will not help us heal. Learning to love ourselves through the wins and challenges of this journey, will.

Chapter 15

NO JUDGMENT

"Sometimes painful things
teach us lessons
that we didn't think we needed to learn."

- AMY POEHLER

*I*F WE WANT TO HEAL ourselves or support others on their journey, we must leave judgment behind and become curious. Asking questions such as "I wonder what I will discover as I'm healing?" and "I wonder what that other person's experience is really like?" help us put our assumptions aside and weave a fabric of shared experience with others.

When we become curious about ourselves and the world around us, others recognize a pattern of empathy in our fabric. They see the tenderness we are wearing, perceive it as a strength, and become attracted to it. These authentic connections of compassion help us discover new pathways to explore the world around us.

Similarly, when we don't ask questions, we may activate our biases and repel others. We interfere with their healing journey when we begin to make purposeless judgments about others and their process. If you want to support others on their journey of empowerment, be curious, not judgmental.

In my opinion, no one has the right to deny another's pain or their healing experience. There is no schedule for healing. I find that the most judgmental people are those who have not forgiven and healed themselves. Heck, it took me a while to acknowledge how the different parts of me - the Inner Children, and the Inner Grown-ups - experienced my traumatic encounters.

For the longest time, I tried to force my Inner Children to heal as if healing could be rostered. I tried to control the process by forcing them to stay in the dark forest until "it was done," but I ended up causing them more anxiety instead. I cracked my healing code when I realized that the optimum healing experience meant learning to visit, linger, and come out of the dark forest fluently.

My traumatized Inner Children were like scared horses. They had to learn that they could visit the dark forest and even dip their toe in the pool of self-condemnation but not stay too long and lose themselves. My Inner Children's confidence grew as I let myself move in and out of the pain and grief without judgment. This process of approach and retreat helped me find a fundamental level of self-love, freedom, and creativity. I discovered that I was loveable and worthy, even with all my flaws.

During this time of emotional repair, I realized that everyone's needs are different:

- Some need to make quick visits to the dark forest.
- Some need to unpack and stay for a while.
- Some take a permanent residence in the dark forest. Their sense of hopelessness and identification with their trauma may stop them from ever leaving.
- And some have decided to stay for good. They attempt to force their loved ones to join them by refusing to heal themselves or let the other person go. Instead, they try to make their healing the responsibility of others. Unless they learn about loving boundaries, people in these

trauma-bonded relationships continue to look for toxic dynamics with others. If their significant other does not follow them to the dark forest, they are likely to find a new person to continue their toxic dynamic with. If they can't find anyone, they end up wandering around the forest aimlessly, not knowing what to do. Their hearts are aching from loneliness as they try to connect with others in a meaningfully trauma-bonded way. In their outward lives, they may seem just as directionless and clueless about their inner power to change their circumstance.

As an Empath, I can't tell you how hard it is to watch some of these dynamics play out. But because I don't get to judge how others live their lives, I can only be curious about their process and wish them well while trusting that their journey is perfect for them. I will help them, but only if they ask for it, and then commit to doing the work.

In my mind, freedom is your birthright. I will support you, even if you choose to stay in the darkness, although I won't join you. I will cheer you on from the sidelines because I've been there. It took humility and genuine effort to rebuild a loving, trustworthy relationship with myself, where I *believed* I was worthy of a life outside the dark forest. Before I could permit myself to leave the darkness, I had to convince my toxic white knight that I could hold the reins of life and that he could trust me to take charge.

When I finally made it out of the forest, I realized how trauma-centric I had become. Those who didn't join me in the forest had moved on with their lives, and those I had met there didn't want me to leave. They wanted me to stay in the darkness by asking me to relive my struggles and, thus, retraumatize myself. I had been a willing audience for their trauma, too. But after the initial feeling of belonging, none of us felt more empowered by staying and continuing to share our stories in a loop. My time in the dark forest was not wasted; it came to a natural end when I realized regurgitating my old story of trauma was no longer serving me.

When I left the dark forest of trauma, I left it with humility. I wanted to set myself up for success because I knew I'd be back for a visit. I learned a lesson I didn't know I needed: I realized the necessity of facing pain. Visiting the dark forest, and knowing my way around it was an essential part of self-witnessing and thus, healing.

After each visit to the dark forest, the light in the outside world seemed a bit brighter. The sun felt good on my skin, and I felt grateful for my growing capacity to travel between the two worlds. Everything became clearer as I learned to move between the trauma and non-trauma realities more fluently. I started seeing my life and what was going around me more clearly. With every transition, I could let go of shame, look into the eyes of those I loved, and withhold my judgment a little bit longer.

I was no longer just staring at my own belly button. Am I judging myself for having been so self-focused? No, because that would be just another way to sabotage my healing. Instead, I treated myself gracefully and kindly as I learned to accept myself and my quirks.

Was the world outside the dark forest all fun and games? Of course not. It was scary and challenging. Is every person outside the dark forest safe? Of course not! But every person isn't a threat either. But I knew that if I wanted to heal, I would have to learn how to take some new risks. Much like many survivors of childhood abuse, I, too, had to learn how to let go of my conditioned mistrust of people. Having stayed with myself through my dark forest episodes, I have realized that even if someone disagrees with me, they are not necessarily a threat to my safety and well-being.

The armor of my white knight had changed color to represent the darkness from which we had emerged together. With my dark warrior next to me, I have learned how to lean into disagreements and even outright aggression. He has taught me to view challenging situations with others as an opportunity to grow in self-trust, and clear and assertive communication.

My dark forest is now reserved for special trips only. I visit it when I need to connect to my pain and grief. I know my way in, and I know my way out again. Because of this ability to navigate my emotional landscape at will, I have come to comprehend my power to direct my emotions. It's a game-changer to recognize that you can stay strong and functional in the face of adversity but stay vulnerable and open with the people you love.

If you want to give yourself and others every opportunity to heal, learn to slow down and become deliberate. Become curious and not judgmental. Take time to step back and think about your dark forest. How often do you want to visit? How long do you want to stay?

Ask these questions of others who feel comfortable sharing with you, too. I suspect you will find that everyone has experienced traumatic events and that every person is unique in how they deal with it. Some embrace the deep work, others don't, and for some, trauma is a complete no-go area! It's important to remember that this is not a game of comparison. This game is called "Sovereign Life," and everyone gets to make their own rules.

Chapter 16

REFLECTIONS

"It's good to be loved but
profound to be understood."

- PORTIA DE ROSSI

ONE OF THE MOST ACCURATE reflections of our self-love is our relationships with others. As a significant portion of marriages ends with divorce, we should consider these two things:

1. Would fewer relationships break down if we became curious instead of being judgemental of our partner and
2. How does our relationship with ourselves contribute to our relationship with our significant other?

In some parts of the world, the divorce rate is nearly fifty percent. Most of these "failed" marriages are doomed because we don't take the time to really know ourselves and bring our best selves to the table. Instead, we may engage in unconscious power struggles. Some of us have also forgotten that both people are sovereign beings, not just an extension of the other.

Many traditional practices pressure people to remain in unhappy or even abusive marriages. In contrast, many modern-day societal trends condition us to take everything personally and get divorced as soon as the relationship's honeymoon period ends. It's like we have come to view the union of marriage either as a fairytale or a trap, instead of an equal partnership of growth. Whether we're talking about a marriage, a civil union, a de-facto partnership or non-labeled, every relationship is as unique as the people in it, and I don't get to judge them. I believe that everyone does the best they can with the self-knowledge, self-love, and relationship skills they possess at that time.

I also believe that when it comes to others' relationships, we would do well to learn some basic boundaries. Remember, our opinion about others' affairs is only that: the lowest form of knowledge. The only people who really know what's going on in a marriage are the people in it - and maybe their therapist. And even then, each person has their own version of the events and their union. I'm about to share my experience with you, and please keep in mind that this is my understanding of what unfolded and not necessarily the whole truth.

I got divorced in my early thirties. In my twenties, I married a kind man who had been a professional athlete, and as his friends relayed the story, he had been very successful. Although he was a hard worker and highly respected by his peers, his promising athletic career ended with an unexpected injury. His sports career, international successes, and game-changing injury all happened years before I met him. His peers' respect for him gave me a sense of who he was in his heart and soul, and I respected him for many of his qualities, including his love for sports.

We were together at the time I purchased Vesper. Soon after she came into my life, I realized I had something extraordinary - a high-potential young horse. My time at Waterside Stud inspired me to specialize in show jumping. I'd already made up my mind, but after my coach insisted I pop over some cross-country fences, my passion for eventing was ignited. With a strong background in dressage, I thought: "Why not?" Each discipline interested me, and Vesper seemed to enjoy and excel in them all.

If you know anything about eventing, you know how all-consuming it is. During the week, I would spend twenty to twenty-five hours at the yard caring for the horses and training with Vesper. On the weekends, I would compete, leaving the house as early as 3:30 a.m. and returning close to midnight. Such was the life of a professional athlete, and I remember thinking how lucky I was to be married to someone who understood my dedication to my sport.

But as the years wore on, it became more and more apparent that there was no space in our relationship for another person with high aspirations for sport. His ship had sailed, and he didn't seem inspired to support me in my audacious goals. I felt that if I wanted his love, presence, and acceptance, I would have to forget my dream of representing Finland in the Olympics and think of my equestrian career as a glorified hobby.

To me, his passivity around my passion felt toxic. I felt trapped by his "realism," which I perceived to keep me grounded in the monotony of shopping on Thursdays and going to bed early so I didn't have to watch the dramatized cable news opinion shows every night. I felt like he was stuck in his dark forest and wanted me to build a life with him there.

I want to be clear: I don't have the right to judge his journey. Ultimately, there's no way I can know his experience because there was no communication about it. Simply what felt like unexpressed expectations. But I respect my ex-husband to this day, and I see the perfection of the connection we shared. He helped me realize what was important to me: my pursuit of high-level performance and self-actualization.

No matter how much you care for someone, the bottom line is that the relationship is only as happy as the individuals within it. A good relationship requires honesty, mutual respect, and reciprocal support, so when I didn't receive those things, I left the marriage in pursuit of a more supportive partnership. I wanted to be seen as who I was: a high performer. I didn't wish my aspirations to remind him of his painful memories, but I also **needed** to be loved for who I was. We both deserved to be seen and loved for exactly who we were.

As I returned from France from a scouting trip for the following year's Young Horse World Championships, I didn't go home. I couldn't because I'd seen my passion reflected back to me while I was away. The incredible horse-rider partnerships that had flown around the cross-country course at 25 miles per hour had set my soul on fire. Their mutual trust and connection spoke a language I understood, and I wondered if others felt that their safe space was on horseback, too.

Being with horses and seeing how far we could go together was the most actual form of my soul's expression at that time. In France, I had been around people who believed in me. There was an understanding that all of us could make it to the top, or at least we could all give it an honest try.

The least we would do in the process was to evolve into the best versions of ourselves. When it was time to go home, I felt sick. I knew that if I walked through that front door, I would be influenced to stay in the status quo and play small. So I couldn't go home.

Chapter 17

EVERYTHING IS NOT FINE

> "I think it's important that we don't
> all have to hold our heads high all
> the time saying everything's fine."
>
> - NICOLE KIDMAN

COULD I HAVE DEALT WITH the challenges in my marriage and the breakup better? Without a shadow of a doubt, I certainly could have. I look back at my thirty-something-year-old self and forgive her for not having the skills or the courage to demand that my ex-husband respect my purposeful goals. I couldn't bring myself to say to him: "this is not enough for me." Instead, I pulled a classic INFJ door slam and did what I could to escape the trap I felt I had fallen into. I might have paused more if I'd known then that history that is not healed is doomed to repeat itself.

The breakdown of this relationship and my subsequent several messy attempts at meaningful connections woke me to the deep childhood pain of not feeling loved, which I had ignored for years. While everything was going well for me professionally, I was unhappy with myself. I'd looked for answers to my happiness outside of myself and failed. Miserably. Multiple times. I also hurt others in this process. For that, I am genuinely sorry.

After my divorce, my personal life went from bad to worse. I've seen this happen to my friends and students, too. When we feel raw and vulnerable and get involved with people too quickly after a breakup, we begin to walk down a very costly path. I had lost my self-respect and joy in connecting and was easily manipulated and deceived. I became increasingly embarrassed about how I let others treat me. I didn't call people out on their lies or set boundaries when they treated me poorly. I remember excusing abusive behavior from others because - I told myself - "they didn't mean it."

As you may know, life reflects back to you all the things you need to learn. I had invited all these painful relationships into my life because I was unwilling to face the pain that was within me. After taking a long, hard look in the mirror and considering the mess I had created, a pattern emerged. It was I who didn't love me. And it was I who tolerated others' poor treatment. I was hurt by others because of my own immature conduct and permeable boundaries.

I admitted to myself that it was all on me: my marriage ending, a subsequent partner gaslighting me, and letting addicts and unstable people into my life. No one else was to blame for the mess I was in. I saw myself in the mirror as a lonely, misunderstood victim. I genuinely thought that no one could fathom how I felt and that there was no way out of the mess. I was keeping secrets and dodging concerned questions from loved ones. It wasn't until my friend Tiina pulled me aside and had a quiet word with me that I remembered my power in the situation. I met her for a coffee - well, that's not true. She was drinking tea while I couldn't finish my massive glass of Sauvignon Blanc fast enough before ordering another one.

Tiina saw my pain and asked what was going on. After listening carefully to my agonizing realization, Tiina took my hand. She reminded me that although I was the common denominator in my struggle, it was not all bad news. She said: "Sure, you created all this pain around you, whether directly or indirectly..." Before I had time to get defensive, she continued, "But you also have the power to change it all."

Her words hit me like a sledgehammer to the chest. She was absolutely right. At that moment, I realized I had a lot to learn. There was a great deal about healthy relationships that nobody had taught me. Sure, my parents had shown me what survival looked like, but until then, it had never occurred to me that life and relationships could be calm and nurturing.

I was tired of struggling in one-sided relationships. I remember thinking there *had* to be more to life than chaos and power games. There and then, I committed to learning all I could about relationships. It was time to become a student of my heart. While I wasn't exactly sure what that looked like, I was positive it was time to allow my heart to be seen and accepted.

The first step I took was to stop isolating myself in shame. I started having honest conversations with others who were going through similar growing pains. Through those conversations, I learned I had some massive gaps in my knowledge. The second step, I realized, was to start asking questions. What else didn't I already know? I identified people with great relationships and began earnest inquiries about their experiences.

In that time of self-study, I must have read fifty books on relationships just to gain a perspective contrary to everything I learned in my youth. I wanted to understand what was "normal" and what was not. I needed to know what was acceptable behavior. I wanted to know what relationship behaviors and expectations were healthy so that I could make more balanced and informed decisions going forward.

Have you ever noticed that whatever you focus on, you get more of? The more I focused on healthy relationships, the more examples I started seeing of them. The models were everywhere, but up to this point, I had missed them entirely. I also realized that in the past, I had even dismissed healthy relating as boring or codependent. Boy, did I learn to shut my mouth, sit down, listen, and learn! To this day, unless I see abuse in others' relationships, I don't interfere in them. I share my opinion only if asked.

Back then, I started focusing on relationships in all areas of my life, including my work. As a massage therapist, my clients spoke to me frankly about their relationship wins and challenges. If they asked for my input, I told them about some of the successful approaches I had learned but had not yet tried for myself.

Although I was single during this time, the knowledge I accumulated from books and other people helped me get a sense of what my clients were going through. When they asked for my opinion, I gave it to them with the disclaimer that I was not a relationship expert. I disclosed upfront that I, too, was in the process of learning to use these tools.

Some clients took it upon themselves to try the approaches we discussed. Eighty percent of the clients noticed a big difference. Their relationships improved, and their bodies started showing higher levels of functional freedom. They exhibited significantly reduced amounts of stress, pain, and inflammation in their bodies. I was gobsmacked. Adding actionable relational conversations to my bodywork made the results for my clients" hearts and bodies exponentially more positive. Intuitively, I had always known about the body-mind connection. Still, this body-heart connection was a completely new discovery for me. I mean, it makes sense if you think about it. When we are happy, we are more relaxed, and the other way around!

But it wasn't just the happy parts of relationships that my clients' bodies were reflecting. I started noticing a clear connection between their negative physical symptoms and past psycho-emotional pain and trauma. I didn't want to believe what I was seeing. It felt too painful for me. I braced myself as I realized that the trauma my clients were feeling was hauntingly familiar to me.

Chapter 18

HEALING CELLULAR MEMORY

"Imagine if we measured success by
the amount of safety that people
felt in our presence."

- JONATHAN LOUIS DENT

BODY MEMORY IS REAL. WE don't have to look at statistics of transplant patients experiencing shadow memories to understand that our bodies hold on to past painful experiences. A renowned psychiatrist, Bessel A. van der Kolk, has dedicated his career to researching the effects of post-traumatic stress since the 1970s. His book, Your Body Keeps The Score, outlines a case for storing and releasing the attachment we continue to carry after a traumatic experience.

Discovering formal studies on cellular memory validated what I already knew in my bones: my body was still carrying the toxic stress from my traumatic childhood experiences. Intuitively, I knew I would never be free from their weight if I didn't take intentional steps to release the memories. I also knew that as long as I kept carrying them around, those memories would poison my attempts to create happy and meaningful relationships.

With this realization, I started looking for help. A dear friend introduced me to a cellular memory-release teacher, and I started attending their workshops. Most of the sessions felt liberating, and I enjoyed being seen as a person beyond my trauma. I remember during a lunch break, we all went to the park nearby and played games from our childhood. At that moment, we were children again. A couple of lonely kids in the park wanted to join us, but their parents told them we were strange. "Grown-ups should not be playing games like that," they said. We didn't care. We were free with no baggage and no agendas, and it was glorious.

At some point, the cellular release work started feeling threatening to me. Actually, it wasn't the work itself. It was some of the people. I felt like basic boundary lines were being blurred, and again I was at the receiving end of unexpressed expectations. At first, I believed when the facilitator told me it was just my past trauma still trying to control me. But when he, under the disguise of a late-night one-on-one session, came on to me, I saw what his work had become: a community that enabled predatory behavior by using shame to control people.

I felt deeply betrayed by his move. I felt like he wanted to be intimate with the child-like, free part of me. I felt sick to my stomach. The situation was a reincarnation of the abuse of my childhood innocence. Once more, life had made me face my unresolved trauma. The pain from my childhood was fully activated in my cells, and I felt as if I was again back in that house of horrors. I felt alone, exposed, and had nowhere to hide. The old narrative that all men are predators surfaced once more.

Life has an excruciating way of checking if we are serious about our healing. In my search for better relationships, I had to face what had happened to me decades before. I could have stopped here and identified as a victim once more. But I had a choice: I could let this jerk win and fall back into my depressed sense of self, or I could stand up to his abuse of power on my way to letting go of my past trauma and the narrative that came with it.

I was staring my childhood pain squarely in the eyes and chose myself. I decided to report the teacher. With that, I discovered a whole new level of self-trust. My self-confidence grew, and I was able to start trusting life - and men - in a whole new way. Maybe I didn't have the luxury to surround myself with safe people. But I knew that whatever life threw at me, I would be safe. After all, I had *me*.

It would have been too easy to vilify the whole concept of the transformation of cellular memory because of this one person and his enablers. Thankfully, I realized I had an opportunity to stop being reactive and throw the baby out with the bathwater. I asked myself: "Can I take the lessons of this work and leave the abusive behavior?" My answer was a resounding "Yes. Yes, I can do that." In that moment, I chose to measure my success in how safe I felt around myself, and made a commitment to share that sense of security with my clients.

I took what I learned about my personal cellular memory work and combined it with my practice of heart-centered bodywork. I'm not going to lie. There were times when I doubted myself. I was watching a new discipline emerge in my orthopedic massage and pain management protocol - one that included releasing any cellular memory pain the client was experiencing.

In the Eastern disciplines, the psycho-somatic approach to our bodies is not a new concept, nor is it considered a placebo effect. Yet, Western mainstream medicine had not even heard about emotional cellular memory back then. It was branded as a woo-woo, airy-fairy pretense, not as the acknowledged holistic approach it has since become.

I found it intolerable that there was an easy-to-address problem and that Western medicine refused to acknowledge it. What was most infuriating was that I had no power to change the system. I decided there and then to keep doing my part, no matter how small. I also chose not to care how much judgment or ridicule I would receive. I would let my clients' results show me how valuable my work was.

As a result of this new commitment, the therapeutic effect of my work shot through the roof. The more compassionate I became, the more effective my work was. The realization that most of us have the same mind, heart, and body problems, just to different degrees, helped me become a better bodyworker and a more effective communicator. Showing my clients how people with shoulders up at their ears cannot relax into healthy relationships around them, and people with chronic back issues invariably experience a lack of support in their lives changed the emotional landscape of their lives. It was like they were getting to know themselves through my interpretation of their bodies. But it was one discovery that really blew my mind. When I discovered that a frozen shoulder in a client showed censored creativity, I witnessed the deep, hidden value of my approach to bodywork.

I had to believe what I saw with my own eyes. An eighty-two-year-old woman overcame her frozen shoulder of ten years in four sessions. Western medicine's answer to her problem was painkillers and cortisone shots. But it wasn't just her physical pain that was stifling her. It was her loneliness and lack of creative expression. She had been a painter and an art teacher who had given up on her discipline. As her shoulder improved, her desire for creativity increased. You may think, "Of course! She was able to paint without pain". I agree, and it would have been easy for me to downplay my work, too, had I not asked more questions.

By becoming curious and listening to her intently, I realized that there was more to her story than the simple cause-and-effect equation of soft tissue manipulation. Her frozen shoulder had only developed after her career had ended, and she had felt cast aside by society. She told me about her recurring nightmare where she was thrown off the school bus to the curb and always landed on *that* shoulder. When she was pain-free and started painting again, her nightmares stopped. Releasing her cellular memory of rejection while rehabilitating her frozen shoulder allowed her to let go of the pain and reclaim her power as an artist once more.

At first, I loved this new discovery phase in my professional life. Every client I saw was nearly as excited about my approach as I was. The amount of infertility my clients and I were able to treat naturally was astonishing. I remember one client's husband thanking me for getting his wife pregnant after the trauma of birthing a stillborn child and several subsequent unsuccessful rounds of IVF. I winked at him and said, "I think you had more to do with it than I did!" We both laughed fiercely as if releasing years of disempowerment and grief from the memory of our cells.

But my deep commitment to my work was partly a distraction from my lonely private life. Sure, none of my workdays were boring, and in fact, every one of them was triumphant. I literally cannot remember a bad workday. But like anything in life, committing to something as a distraction and without the appropriate boundaries will inevitably invite you to visit the dark forest.

After a while, I got exhausted from the busyness of work. The massive wins started to feel like never-ending quests for validation because I had no one to share my triumphs with after the day was done. Of course, client confidentiality would have stopped me from disclosing any specifics. Still, I realized I was missing something I had never experienced: a partner asking me how my day went. In essence, I had no way, nor a safe space, to unwind and clear the psychic residue my intense day had left in my cellular memory.

It felt like my clients brought their traumas to me, and I helped release them and then got stuck with their pain. Because of my fears of not being loveable, I held onto their trauma as a trophy or affirmation of my worth. I carried their traumas with me because I wanted to feel special and didn't want to admit that my home was empty. At least others' trauma would keep me company. If I were to let go of the burden, I would have to admit I was lonely. I was damned if I did, and damned if I didn't.

Chapter 19

STOP FIGHTING YOURSELF!

"As long as you keep secrets
and suppress information,
you are fundamentally at
war with yourself."

- BESSEL A. VAN DER KOLK

I REALIZED I NEEDED HELP AND went to therapy. I learned that I was conditioned to be sensitive to others' emotions so that I would stay safe. If I could read my father's moods, I could prevent getting hurt. I could run or make myself small, so maybe he, or people in his orbit, would leave me alone. I had taken this pattern from my childhood and superimposed it onto my adult life and everyone I dealt with. I found myself constantly scanning for my clients' and teammates' emotional landscape to determine their needs. In a way, that's what made me such a great massage therapist.

Therapy helped me understand why work is not a healthy replacement for loving relationships. As a professional person, I was a tool, not a person. As a professional, I was there to do a job. The more work I did, the more output I had. I was giving care, attention, and meaningful connection at work without having the balance of receiving the same in my personal life. I had to learn to refill my cup outside of work.

While working through this pain was hard, it taught me how to use one of the most effective personal development tools: outside input. The fact is that we only know what we know. If we want to grow, we need external input. As a traditionally introverted person, I had only relied on self-study and inner strength to get through hard times. While continuous study, self-reliance, and introspection are essential, so is having the wisdom to know when you've reached the end of your internal capacity to cope. No amount of repetitive articles and well-meaning but ineffective videos will get us out of the echo chamber of our already-established biased thoughts about healing.

My psychotherapist showed me that if I keep repeating the same thoughts and feelings in a never-ending loop, I keep bringing about the same results. I understood I needed to acquire new, **relevant** knowledge instead of dancing around my blind spots forever. I also needed to apply my new skills for something to change. It may sound strange, but that's when the penny dropped for me: like many children of narcissistic parents, I had continued to see myself as an extension of others' lives instead of living my own. I had an extraordinary skill set around staying out of trouble but no knowledge of how to build something I wanted.

So, I decided to learn some new skills: asking for help and sharing my personal self with others. Wow, it was hard! Anyone who has experienced my kind of childhood can tell you that learning these skills directly threatens our sense of security. As children, we are taught that the only way to stay safe is to be a side character in the life of our abusive parent. Being yourself and having your own thoughts was dangerous and potentially fatal.

Through therapy, I discovered that others had overcome the type of pain I was experiencing, and that I could, too. I learned that the way to dig myself out of this hurt was to ask for help and share what was going on without fear of narcissistic retaliation and rage. Ultimately, this time with my therapist showed me that most people were actually safe.

This realization changed the course of the rest of my life. Human beings need each other. We need each others' fresh perspectives so we don't stay stuck in our old story of trauma. If we isolate ourselves from the input of trusted others, we can become radicalized by our own thoughts. As long as I was isolating myself, I genuinely believed that it was not safe to be me and that I was as unloveable as my father had taught me. My time in therapy showed me that it wasn't just me struggling with my self-worth. My subjective emotional experience was universal, and I learned that we could develop a deep sense of belonging by relating to each other through our shared experiences.

If one person struggles with a specific issue, you can almost guarantee that others do, too. In essence, the whole of humankind can connect through pain and healing. Just like we come together around music or sports events, we could come together through overcoming our struggles. While I didn't know it then, this thought of coming together would radically shape my vocational aspirations in years to come.

Like I always do, I took my personal healing experiences and shared them with those who asked for help. Spurred on by my newly found boundaries and insights, I wanted to share a message of compassion, hope, and healing beyond my work as a massage therapist. I chose to share this message with other women struggling with their self-care, self-establishment, and boundaries in relationships.

What would the world look like if we stopped pretending like life is easier than it is and simply showed up as we are? Would we be more open to witnessing one another's experience? Would we have a deeper level of compassion for one another? Could we support one another in a much more profound and effective way?

The idea of women worldwide connecting through a shared healing journey felt revolutionary to me, although I knew it wasn't an original thought. But I felt the concept was powerful, and I wondered how it could be implemented globally. I knew that if I wanted to create greater change, the most important thing was to get organized.

This was how the Radiant Woman movement was born. I started in the mid-2000s by hosting small get-togethers at my bodywork clinic. After a while, we were online and global. We discussed stress management through self-care, self-love, and healthy relationships. One of the most popular topics was "Your Self-Care Matters," which asserted that women's needs and self-care are their central driving force. It's a well that when full, will nourish those around us whom we care about.

If us women don't look after ourselves, how can we look after those we invite into our inner circle? I asked questions like: "Who can you rely on to look after you?" and "What kind of self-care are you modeling for those who look up to you? Are you teaching them to respect themselves or to neglect themselves?"

These were pointed questions, but most of the women wanted to hear them straight. They craved honesty because they were tired of lying to themselves. They felt I had their backs because they knew my questions ultimately came from a place of championing *their* well-being. They trusted me, and I trusted them.

Initially, taking my painful experiences and turning them into powerful questions and conversation starters was scary. My fear of backlash and judgment subsided when I saw the results for the women around me. Once more, I had to release my fears because the evidence in front of me did not align with my trauma-based pained experiences. I've always been a private person, and I could have kept my personal insights about self-love and relationships to myself. But, on the other hand, if my experiences can help one other person heal, it's worth taking the risk of ridicule and punishment.

I know some will be upset with my writing, and I don't pretend to have all the answers or give a picture of perfection. I have always been a perfectly imperfect person, and I am good with that. Making mistakes is an excellent learning opportunity; if you discover how to laugh at yourself, you'll never run out of things to laugh about! But that doesn't mean that I don't get scared. I do, but I take action anyway.

We can share our true selves more openly when we don't have to pretend we are perfect. Communicating our insights with others is much easier when we learn to understand and express ourselves. Self-compassion and expression help us build deep and meaningful relationships with others, maybe even for the first time.

If we fight ourselves and deny our needs and desires, we become unclear about what's important to us and thus contribute to interpersonal misunderstandings. When we show up knowing who we are, we bring an undeniable presence along with us. It's much easier to communicate ourselves, our needs, and our desires directly when we know and love ourselves.

Teaching women to claim and present themselves as the incredible beings they are has been one of the greatest pleasures of my life. It has freed thousands of women across the world to be their powerful selves. These women have stopped putting up with people and situations that are not right for them. And most of all, it has helped them love and care for themselves. As their well runs over, they take better care of the critical people in their lives. Every woman should have a rite of passage where they wholly claim who they are and learn to live unapologetically and with deep love.

The Radiant Woman movement was just a starting point for my global empowerment work. My work has morphed from the pure discipline of physical pain management into empowering people's minds, hearts, bodies, and lives.

By overcoming my own trauma and sharing my learnings, I have taught my students how to lovingly face their pain and not turn away from it. I have shown thousands of people how to put down the cards life dealt them and pick up the cards they want instead. In the early days of the Radiant Woman work, I could not have imagined running a global online academy for healing, personal development, and self-mastery. I mean, I hardly knew how email worked!

But here I am. A lifelong learner still guiding others on their journeys of empowerment. When we stop fighting ourselves, we begin to build a more joyous, compassionate, creative, and effective world for us and future generations. And we get to do it together.

Chapter 20

ARE YOU LIVING DELIBERATELY?

"Healing begins with deciding
that we matter.
Personal Development begins
with a yearning for a better life.
Being a life-long learner brings
about Personal Mastery."

- MERJA SUMILOFF

*W*HERE DOES YOUR PERSONAL EMPOWERMENT start?

Becoming deliberate about what you want to create.

The journey of personal empowerment is like a road trip you take across the globe of your life. Where you are right now is the perfect starting point. Having an idea of where you want to go is advantageous, although not necessary for a fulfilling and meaningful trip. Some of the most profound journeys came from the commitment to explore without a plan and restraint.

Whether you know where you're going, or you simply want to explore life organically, I recommend you make some preparations for your journey.

1. **Ensure your car is in good nick** and you have the right tires for the trip. I liken the condition of your vehicle to the

health of your body. Just like you would not expect your car to go far on punctured tires, your body needs nourishment from you. Paying attention to the basics of your life: sleep, healthy food, hydration, and functional fitness will prevent breakdowns during your journey to self-discovery.

2. **Have enough fuel for your journey.** Living in tune with your values helps you fuel your car. If you don't live according to your values, you run out of enthusiasm for your journey. Toxic positivity won't help you here. No matter how many "happy face" stickers you put on top of an empty fuel gauge, they won't fill the tank. Suppose you don't connect your day-to-day activities to your personal values. In that case, you will eventually feel like you are not living your own life but only exist as an appendix for someone else.

3. **Pick your route according to your vehicle.** Your car is like your cognitive preference. Each of us prefers to make decisions predominantly by feeling or thinking. Do you have an off-roader who enjoys life's emotional roller-coasters or a smart city car that is focused on efficiency and effectiveness?

   a. If you're a predominant feeler, you will naturally focus on the emotional aspects of your journey. Thus, you'll have a car that can handle your trip's inevitable emotional ups and downs. You'll also base most of your decisions on how they make you, or people around you, feel. But squeezing this off-roader into a height-restricted parking garage won't work. If you are a natural feeler, don't try only to think your way through life. You can exercise critical thinking while learning to harness the power of your emotions. Your healthy emotional landscape will be the best guide for your journey!

105

b. If you are a predominant thinker, you naturally go for effectiveness and fuel economy. Your car will likely be the most fuel-efficient and practical vehicle for reaching the destination. You will make most of your decisions on what is reasonable and makes sense. Forcing this car off-road into the emotional landscape of feelings will likely damage the chassis or wear out its engine. That doesn't mean you can't listen to music that gets you into your feelings. By all means, do garnish your journey with emotional touch points! But remember to focus primarily on staying on the road you planned, taking the turns that make the most sense to you, and enjoy your trip!

When you respect your natural decision-making talents, your journey to empowerment becomes more authentic and pleasurable. By embracing the car you are in, you'll avoid going down wrong roads and having unnecessary inconveniences disguised as flat tires and parking tickets. Are you a predominant feeler or thinker? Reach out to the Sumiloff Academy if you need support in finding out.

4. **Be clear about your starting point:** find yourself on the map. Understanding your values, natural talents, and cognitive functioning is not enough to give you a solid starting point for your journey. It would help if you also had a map. This map is your current life as it is in its actualized form. Instead of showing the Chesapeake Bay with its names changed, your life map will reflect the status of your relationships, living arrangements, vocation, and finances. Starting from where you are, what skills do you have or need to learn to complete your personal

empowerment journey? Being realistic about your current circumstances will help you prepare for the trip.

5. **Understand why you are leaving.** Are you taking the trip to grow and explore or to run away from an uncomfortable situation? If you are looking to grow, great news! Since you will be bringing yourself with you, you'll have plenty of opportunities to evolve on this trip to your personal empowerment. But if you are leaving because you want to escape your current life, remember that you are the one who created it. No amount of personal empowerment work will change your circumstances if you are not taking full responsibility for your current starting point. Understand why you are leaving, because you cannot escape yourself.

Deciding to change your life will allow you a clean slate. However, owning your current circumstances before starting your trip will help you take a more sober, gradual approach to your personal evolution. Balancing yourself before taking off means that your travel companion (you) will be more relaxed and pleasurable to be around. Have you ever been on a long road trip with an angry or resentful person? I sure have. It's uncomfortable to spend hours in a confined space with a person who is upset. Don't do that to yourself. Own your starting point and find some balance in your life before taking off, and the trip will be much less chaotic.

Once you are ready for your trip to create a more empowered life, it's time to pick the destination. Your destination can be a specific goal or an exploratory trip in a generally chosen direction. For example, you can create a plan to become a better listener to your partner or be open to learning different communication styles in relationships. Whether your destination is specific or general, it'll be right for you.

Don't compare your destination to that of others. What you want from life is right for you. Own it. Being conscious about what you do and don't want to achieve in your life is like deciding on your rest stops. There is no "right route" to take on this pilgrimage to your empowerment. Rest when you need to, and keep going when you're ready to continue your self-exploration. I believe that all of our journeys are as unique as we are.

As much as we sometimes wish to find a generic, predetermined route, I would hate for you to settle for less than you deserve. That's why I recommend you aim for your dream life, no matter how unrealistic it may seem at the start of your journey. You may not achieve everything you want, but if you work consistently and patiently toward your goals, you will be much further along than if you simply decide your dreams are unachievable.

If you're unsure which direction to go, start somewhere and take a short day trip to see if you want to continue further. For example, trying out a new communication style with a friend can show you if it feels right and authentic to you. If you are unsure, there's no need to commit to a whole articulation system upfront. Try it, and if you like it, keep going!

Sometimes, your journey feels as easy as cruising in the fast lane. An unexpected happenstance can feel like a puncture and may set you back temporarily. It's ok. Park safely, change your tire and get your speed back. It pays well to use the power of the pause when things don't go how we imagined they would. It's a rare incident that stops us altogether. Most of the time, we can fix the problem and keep going.

Perhaps you've noticed that the best routes don't always work out and that life can show you an unexpected shortcut just when you think you know where you are going. Don't fret. Changing your plan mid-trip is entirely normal. You don't have to know precisely how the rest of your life will play out.

When your trip changes unexpectedly, it can bring about your old habits of disempowerment. I was in my thirties when I abruptly moved to Australia. For the first six months, I didn't work. While initially great, this lack of goals and focus eventually led me to my old people-pleasing habits. When I caught myself constantly putting others' needs first, I stopped. I took a step back and decided to course-correct. I decided to restart my intentional journey into self-study and empowerment in this new world my decision to leave Ireland had created. Initially, I was uncertain about my self-development goals and even the general direction I wanted to take. But I knew I should start doing something just for me. I took a day trip to a place I knew I would enjoy: horses.

I started hanging out with horses and riding with my new friends, and we even rescued three horses from the local RSPCA. The process of adoption was a highly emotional journey for me. I missed my Irish horses, but knew they were well looked after by one of my students and her husband. The horses we adopted in Australia reminded me of who I was in my heart of hearts, and I could not have been more grateful for the privilege. It felt like these rescue horses had come about just in time to remind me of my inner power and direction.

One of my dear rescue horses, Wiraki Velocity HSH
(Red Horse), and I on the beach in Australia.

As it always does, the universe delivers another opportunity to be happy when you start doing something you love. Adopting the horses opened up my heart to more creativity and vitality. I started reading more. When I came across several personal development blogs, I knew in my gut that I was on to something. I remember whispering: "What is this MBTI?". I set myself a goal of reading the blogs to understand my personality type better. I didn't know exactly what all the technical jargon meant, but I was ready to learn. Adopting the horses had helped me break the pattern of putting others first, and as I returned to myself, I became a student of my life.

Because of the tone of some of the articles, I genuinely thought that personality development tools like Myers-Briggs Type Indicator® and Enneagram were created to point out everything that was wrong with me. Boy, was I wrong! Of course, some people with limited knowledge of the tools use them to tear themselves or others down. But when I put these tools to work, I was pleasantly surprised. Because I only worked with qualified practitioners, I got the right end of the stick. They helped me see what was **right** with me. I felt seen - by someone else - as my own sovereign being, not just a servant to others. My mind blew open, and although, at the time, I wasn't aware of this shift either, the vocational direction of my life continued to grow further into the field of personal empowerment.

Powered by this discovery, I gained the confidence to keep learning. My days were filled with self-study and chilling with the horses. Horses had - once more - come to show me the way. It's like they had the power to slow down my mind so that I could capture the lessons I needed to learn. My journey to self-mastery started taking shape as I slowly - and sustainably - moved from one significant realization to another. With the help of this lifestyle, **I realized that my childhood abuse was not my fault and that it was my responsibility to set aside the guilt and shame I had been carrying for decades.**

My journey to my new life in Australia brought me to many crossroads of choice. If I wanted a pleasurable trip, I had to pause before deciding which turn to take. Putting down the map of a victim and picking up one of the survivors was hard at first. My hand was so used to reaching for the old story that it felt like learning the new habits was taking forever. Whenever I had to decide about a relationship, job, or finances, I would have to slow down, pull over, and consciously pick up the correct map. Only then, I could start navigating the roads again. Sure, I had a choice of turning the car around and returning to the comfort of the old story of being a victim. Or I could use pulling over and pausing as an opportunity to reinforce my newly remembered inner power. Most often, I chose to take a risk and keep driving forward to the unknown, uncharted territories.

Consciously choosing to drive away from my victimhood served me well. I knew to keep my car in good nick by nurturing my physiology. I fueled my car by living according to my values. I drove the car I had, making the most of my cognitive talents. I understood my starting point and what I wanted to change. And I knew why I was leaving: I wasn't running away from my painful past but traveling toward an empowered future.

What about you? Do you know where you are in life? Are you making deliberate choices about your destination or simply letting life move you around? How conscious are you of your decisions when you hit a crossroads of choice? If your life feels like a mess, and you can't answer these questions, it's okay. I want to remind you to take one step at a time. You are a sovereign being with the right to choose your own journey. Can you pause for a moment and remember your inner power to choose? What's something small you can do today to start your journey toward more empowerment?

If you need support, join us at the Sumiloff Academy: Sumiloff.com

Chapter 21

SHARING YOURSELF WITH OTHERS

"Don't you ever let a soul
in the world tell you
that you can't be exactly who you are."

- LADY GAGA

INITIALLY, MY SELF-EMPOWERMENT JOURNEY FELT selfish because I was conditioned to consider others first. But I persisted. The old conditioning of only living for others took a while to shake, but I knew that if I wanted to really know myself, I would have to keep going. I committed to failing forward, pausing, and forgiving myself for not being perfect as I learned new ways of being and communicating.

I wanted those I loved and respected to understand who I was becoming. Trying to communicate the unknown "becoming" to others was nearly impossible, but I kept going. I knew I didn't want to overwhelm them with a firehose of insight and new understanding I was gaining every day. I wanted to be kind, considerate, and concise in my communications. It was like writing and sending thoughtful postcards from my deep travels to those I cared about.

As I was writing, I had to be concise with my message because, much like real postcards, too much information in a limited space will end up muddying the waters. I also had to be intentional about my core message. Was I looking to connect, update, or challenge the other person? Could I say what I meant, and could I mean what I said?

One day, after a particularly delicious meditation session, I realized that we, in societies, are not conditioned to share our personal journeys openly and succinctly. We are taught to hide our innermost thoughts, feelings, desires, and needs. Many of us are scared to stand out in case we get ridiculed or attacked.

Too many children are taught to fit into the mold of "the right way of being." Many of us are not encouraged to explore our values, needs, natural gifts, and cognitive capacities, nor are we taught how to communicate them confidently.

When we permit ourselves to take off the blinkers of "who we should be," we discover our innate genius and begin to show up as a more empowered version of ourselves. Every person's self-discovery genius is a little different, but to avoid going down any rabbit holes, indulge me as I use some cognitive categories here.

Some of us are more introverted, and others are more extroverted. Knowing this is very helpful when you need to tap into your natural energy source or intentionally replenish yourself after a challenging week. Do you need time to yourself, or does connecting with others give you energy?

Some of us prefer a tactile learning environment, while others need time to visualize their plan before taking action. Knowing your information-collection and ordering style is vital to finding the right teachers and maximizing your learning journey.

When making crucial decisions, some prefer to stick to the facts. In contrast, others have an uncanny capacity to tune into people's emotional landscapes. Thinking and feeling are essential cognitive functions we can utilize in sound decision-making. The more practiced your cognitive skills are, the better your decisions about life, love, health, and wealth.

Some people discover their inner genius through intellectual pursuits, while others use relationship-oriented learning through conversations and shared experiences. There are those of us who strive toward a meaningful vision and others who simply trust life to show us what we need to learn. Some of us pick up patterns that open up new intuitive discoveries, and others work best with traditional mentoring from those who have walked the path before them. Whatever your primary self-discovery genius is, it is valid and valuable. You see, there is more than one way of learning, and your natural preference is the perfect starting point for you.

As much as our cognitive capacities differ, so do our personal values. What are the things you value in life? How we fill our days can give us clues about what is important to us in life. Peter Hagerty, whom I mentioned earlier, asks his clients to list what they spend most of their money and time on. He then invites his clients to discover the essence behind their answers.

For example, a mother of three spends most of her income on her mortgage. Is her top value paying the bank man? I doubt it. It's much more likely that she wants a safe and predictable place where her children can grow up without uprooting in the middle of the process.

Learning to identify and communicate your values to others in a caring and concise way is profoundly healing. As you discover yourself and learn to share your values with others, you begin to own what is important to you. In the process, you also learn how to strengthen your authentic voice. Communicating your values to those around you can also teach them how to trust and respect you. This helps them see you and love you on a deeper level.

When we get to know who we are and share our authentic selves with others, our world gets less chaotic and unpredictable. Others can honor you more proactively as they understand your intent and what drives you. Misunderstandings, miscommunication, and misrepresentations also begin tapering off gradually. While it may take some time to iron out any past miscommunications, when you really care for someone, it is work worth doing. Remember, ignorance breeds chaos. If we don't make the effort to know and communicate our needs and values clearly and succinctly, we can't blame others when they don't understand us or misinterpret our intentions.

Understanding our natural gifts, preferred decision-making styles, and values doesn't only help us with our relationships. This knowledge and skill set will also help us navigate life's crossroads, especially when we are not sure what decision to make. Instead of constantly second-guessing ourselves or pleasing others to stay safe, we get to choose a direction, knowing that no matter what happens, we will be okay. This will help us make the most of life's opportunities and build an existence that looks more like our authentic selves. Showing up and sharing ourselves with others authentically allows us to choose what kinds of relationships, financial arrangements, and life circumstances we want to create on our own and with others.

Knowing yourself and those important to you is deeply consequential. Without a profound understanding of ourselves and those that are important to us, we are doomed to live a life of loneliness or relational turmoil. Sharing ourselves with others meaningfully and encouraging them to do the same creates deep connections and clarity about our purposeful lives.

Chapter 22

HOW YOU SHOW UP, MATTERS

"Your energy has the power
to change the vibe
of every room you enter."

— MERJA SUMILOFF

AUTHENTIC RELATIONSHIPS REQUIRE RAPPORT, AND rapport starts with communication. We build our relationships on a series of positive or negative interactions with others, and our trust and intimacy grow or reduce accordingly.

How we show up in our relationships with others determines the outcome of those relationships. The more intentional, positive interactions we have with our partner, the more favorable outcome is probable. The opposite is also true. We can't expect a positive outcome if we only bring negativity to our relationships. Every child of baby boomers knows exactly what I mean. So many of our parents were never taught how to speak to each other in a supportive and caring way. It seems like their generation was doomed to live in a relationship power struggle indefinitely.

In contrast, I think the boomer relationships were saved by their commitment to action. After all, it's not just what we say but also what we do. Yes, words are essential, and it's a very good idea to consider them before speaking, but ultimately, words are an expression of an intent that only actions can prove right or wrong. Say what you want about the boomers' lack of positive communication, their commitment to action for the common good speaks for the power of this incredible generation. Do you know someone who shows up in a chaotic situation and remains calm and collected? It could be a family member, teacher, preacher, or local firefighter. Their response to your crisis can determine how you feel about them in the future.

Let me give you a personal example. If you know me, you know I am an animal lover. I want all animals to be well, safe, and happy. But if you have had animals, you also know the duty of care and the inevitable pain of the loss. Our dear neighbors left to travel, and I stepped up to look after their livestock while they were away. Two days in, one of their chickens sustained internal injuries from what seemed like an egg that had gotten stuck in her birthing vent. She suffered grave harm, and it was clear that she would not make it to the vet, even if I took her straight away. I had a decision to make, and how I showed up in this challenging situation mattered.

I called my neighbor and explained what had happened and the extent of the old girl's injuries. My neighbors knew this would be distressing for me because they knew my love for animals. They hesitantly asked if I would quickly release the chook from her pain by performing euthanasia at home. I told them" Yes" and that I would let them know when it was done.

Like with every death I have encountered to date, I stayed present with the chook and thanked her for her incredible contributions to happiness and eggs. I let her spirit move on quickly and humanely. I had a swift cry and messaged my neighbor to say that the old girl was gone and that the rest of the chooks looked fine. My neighbor texted me back, appreciating my efforts and thanking me for my pragmatic approach to resolving the issue.

My neighbors had faced a painful situation with no power over it. Still, they found great comfort in having a reliable person caring for their beloved friends. After I handled this tough act of mercy for them and their animals, I felt like they saw me in a different, more positive light. While this story illustrates my point well, building better relationships doesn't have to be a question of life and death. Much trust and respect can be earned by simply being present with others as they face life's challenges and joys.

I encourage you to look back at challenging situations where you stepped up to the plate and did the right thing, especially when it was hard.

- Did you stand up for someone who wasn't in the room while another person was misrepresenting them?
- Did you stay present with a friend as she was grieving her divorce after being left for a younger woman?
- Have you taken leadership of a chaotic situation, even though you knew you could get hurt in the process?
- Did you face a difficult conversation with a loved one, knowing it would cause them, or you, pain?

All humans are created equal, and our energy, outlook, and presence have the power to grow or destroy our relationships. I sure know what it feels like to be at the receiving end of someone else's whims, but I must remember that we all have that power. Everyone can show up positively or negatively to any situation - regardless of anyone else's conduct. The question is: do we take the time to choose our response, or do we simply react?

Had I run from the difficult task of helping our neighbor's chicken in her passing, I would not have felt very good about myself, and I doubt I would have been asked to look after their livestock again. Although the experience was distressing for me, I did what had to be done.

We all experience tough times, and sometimes, staying positive and productive is impossible. This is entirely normal and valid. We are not robots of positivity. I've seen thousands of students struggle with loss, abuse, unexpected life changes, and copious amounts of psycho-emotional pain. Pretending that everything is fine when it's not reduces others' trust and respect toward us. They, especially if highly intuitive, know when we are faking it. Just be gentle with yourself and others as you - and they - work with the hodge-podge of energy we all create together. Do your best to communicate your internal process of struggle without lashing out or placing blame.

Our resilience to face difficult situations grows with this authentic connectedness. Does it mean that simply knowing about this energy exchange will automatically change it? Yes and no. Yes, acknowledging this dynamic is essential, but if you want to be fluent in your energetic contribution, you must practice. Putting yourself into difficult situations and practicing staying energetically positive will inevitably create a valuable success habit for you. Even when we don't get it perfect, doing our best to mind the energy we bring to our interactions will make a difference. Over time, and with our best efforts, we will learn to give and receive support as we move through tough times with others.

In contrast, those who don't take responsibility for their energetic exchanges live in a world of chaos. Their outlook in life is bleak as they hope the next person will make them feel whole, only to find out that it's not possible. Some of these people have completely given up on hope for genuine connections with others. They wander into the dark forest, never to be seen again. They may be living their lives in physical terms but not be present with any of their relationships, jobs, or activities. This isolated way of living is stressful and can lead to adopting coping mechanisms such as substance abuse and compulsive behavior. These displaced behaviors are used in an attempt to cope with life while feeling a deep sense of loneliness.

But helping others with their loneliness is not as simple as deciding to connect with them. If you attempt to block their travel to the dark forest, the person struggling to connect can become reactive or even abusive. Some people simply need to be left to it. For too long, I tried to keep others from entering the dark forest because I didn't trust they could manage their time there productively. But I was actually projecting onto them my father's inability or unwillingness to heal himself and find his way out. I had become so conditioned to perform emotional judo on others' pain that I started practicing the exact thing I was trying to heal from: Control over others.

I genuinely thought that I was the only person that could help or save them. How presumptuous of me. Yes, it was true that my father never found his way out of the dark forest and that he controlled me by blaming me for making him go there. According to him, it was I, who had ruined his life by simply just being born. But as I healed, developed, and progressively mastered my life, I realized that others' journeys weren't mine to control. My life became much lighter when I stopped trying to control them by "keeping them happy" and focused on my own healing journey.

While I have lost significant people to the dark forest, I don't get to have an opinion about their journey. I don't get to judge them because of how and when or if they ever want to come out of the forest. However, I do get to make that choice about my journey.

Yes, addictions, displaced behavior, and unhealed grief and trauma can break relationships. But so can our controlling ways. If we don't give others the freedom to walk their own journey and learn their own lessons, we contribute to their heartache. This doesn't mean that a significant other's addiction gets to dictate *your* life. There's a balance between supporting others and giving them space to grow. It's not just the addict that needs to make sober decisions. It's the people around them, too. If we are sober about the consequences of our and others' actions, we all can set loving boundaries accordingly.

When we heal, we may realize that our primary connection point with those around us is through pain, control, or disconnect. This is called trauma bonding. When we connect with others in this way, both people involved must grow for the relationship to survive. In the same way, we can't control others and their journey. We should not attempt to force this process of growth on them. Instead, we can seek to inspire others by sharing our own journey of evolution. By learning how to ask for your needs to be met without apologizing, you may influence others to do the same.

Chapter 23

YOUR NEEDS ARE IMPORTANT

"We are not under obligation to
keep it together for others
while feeling as if we are
falling apart inside."

- NATALIE LUE

LEARNING TO IDENTIFY AND ASK for your needs to be met is integral to authentic and healthy relationships. If you're anything like me, you may have been putting your own needs aside to avoid appearing needy or high maintenance. Personally, I used to put up with too many inconveniences in fear of being judged. I was afraid that by asking for my basic needs to be met, I would drive those I loved out of my life because I felt I was asking for too much.

Of course, my fear of being left is not set in the reality of *healthy* relationships. What healthy person would judge me for wanting to have an ordered and clean home? I'm not talking about being obsessive about the house. I want a calm environment and no grittiness of sand under my bare feet as I go to the kitchen to get a cup of ridiculously strong coffee.

Those who love us want us to feel fulfilled so that we can be comfortable and happy. And those who see basic needs as "high maintenance" really are not worth building a life with. They are likely to perpetuate your sense of insignificance by asserting microaggressions around your needs until you break, or one of you gets fed up with the situation.

If you are used to being in one-sided relationships, even the thought of setting boundaries can feel threatening. While this is entirely normal, you can slowly but surely dig yourself out of that hole of self-sacrifice. Recognizing and voicing your needs and the subsequent boundaries is a skill that can be learned over time and with practice. You may think: "easier said than done."

You are right. None of this is easy, especially if we have fears based on experiences of abuse, abandonment, or betrayal. I hear you, and I see you. Yes, it's hard, and you're so worth the work!

You may think I'm minimizing or marginalizing your trauma, or saying that you should hide your worst emotions. In fact, what I'm saying is exactly the opposite. I believe visiting the dark forest is crucial. Much like the occasional camping trip in real life by airing your emotions, you can reset your body clock, feel more connected to nature and relax. Giving your grief and trauma some space and fresh air can help you return to your personal "neutral."

I would even go as far as to say that befriending grief and trauma can lead to a swift healing experience and a positive thrust forward in life. A balanced life has both struggles and hope. Experiencing both with those around you is a great way to build a lasting, sustainable, and reciprocal bond. The most meaningful and deep relationships are ones where both peoples' needs are met through the good and bad times. Remember to discover and learn to voice your needs with those you love so that your relationships stay balanced, especially when times are tough.

As you can see, knowing yourself is not enough for us humans. To be happy, we must also understand how to relate to others as our authentic selves. It is a rare person who can have a happy and meaningful life alone. Thus, learning to connect and have conversations about both positive and challenging topics, such as your needs, can deepen your level of intimacy with others.

Intimacy, even if platonic, is essential when we want to experience meaningful connections and a deep sense of belonging.

Belonging is not just about tribalism and ideological echo chambers. For example, I find this current political and psycho-social climate of competition and what-about-ism lacking in accountability and a real sense of belonging. When I get asked about my political beliefs, I reply, "They are private," or "I believe in people, not politics." The need I'm fulfilling with these answers is to stay connected with people well beyond political beliefs.

If we buy into political tribalism instead of learning to communicate our needs effectively, we contribute to a world of chaos where our politicians are driven by fame, and not their service for those who elected them. Most peoples' issues would be resolved if our politicians would stop behaving like petulant teenagers, and grow into the representatives they are elected to be. Remember, we are the ones who have to hold our representatives accountable for their performance.

By not taking ownership of our energy, we give our power away. Even when we disagree, we don't have to add to everyone's pain. Are you able to hear others' views without getting triggered? If not, you buy into your own flavor of tribalism, and the deeper you go, the harder it is to get out. If we keep going further down the echo chamber, then it's just a matter of time before those we thought were in our tribe turn on us, too. After all, I'm yet to meet two people who agree on everything.

When we are too busy telling others our opinions, we don't listen. When others talk *at* us, we *don't want to* listen. They may have real needs, but the power struggle around who is "right" overrides a beneficial outcome. By ignoring others' needs, we sow seeds of mistrust in those relationships. Too many of us don't really listen to understand where others are coming from. Learning to ask thoughtful questions can open a window to others' souls. If we want to build reciprocal and authentic relationships, we must stop listening to others so that we can respond. We must learn to listen to them so that we can understand. At this stage, you may think, "But Merja, what about me?!"

That's right, you, too, are essential. That's why I'm encouraging you to discover your needs, learn to share them lovingly and normalize thoughtful disagreements within your circle of influence. It's completely okay for two people to disagree and still get along. Normalizing different perspectives can teach others to consider you, too. Exemplifying mature behavior and holding others accountable for their promises is more powerful than forcing others to change. If you stick to connecting with others in this meaningful way and they don't want to respect your differing outlook, they will inevitably move on to relationships that feel more comfortable for them.

Why are we still putting up with power struggles and bad behavior? Why don't we make it a **standard** to have respectful and curious communications with the people we love and respect - even if we disagree? If our conditioning teaches us to compete for attention, why not turn that ship around? Deliberately normalizing positive interactions with others - especially those who disagree with you - will not take anything away from you. In fact, it brings more joy and meaning into your life. Kindness, compassion, and success are not finite resources, and as such, don't have to be withheld from others, especially those important to you.

But I get it: being real and asking for your needs to be met is scary. It is much safer and easier to be defensive than openly vulnerable. Most people don't ask questions but try instead to protect themselves and their opinions. Sadly, they simply don't want to take the risk of being wrong or getting hurt. These people believe that being "right" protects them. But it's not real safety. It's their toxic ego stopping them from having authentic experiences with others.

Racism is a perfect example of this. The number of white supremacists who are afraid to meet a person of color up close is convincing - and disturbing. I guess the old adage is true: it's easy to hate from afar. It takes fierce courage to tear down your walls, meet "the other," and ask earnest questions. It takes guts to keep going when you're scared to find out that you may be wrong. It takes grace to allow yourself to fail and start again. As with all potential negative interactions, it takes great daring to be vulnerable.

Let's turn our attention to the relationship with our significant other. Most people are not used to hearing or giving positive feedback after the relationship's honeymoon phase has passed. It can be frightening to tell someone you admire, care for, love, or respect them, especially if you have been drifting apart for a while or have been thinking about leaving the relationship.

Vulnerability is hard. Authenticity is hard if you're not used to it! The bottom line is that deepening our relationships through vulnerability and authenticity takes courage. And these connections start with uncomfortable conversations, whether positive or negative. Let's try this together. Pick a safe person and tell them something you like or admire about them. If I were doing this with you right now, I could say, "I don't know if you know this, but I am incredibly impressed by your willingness to see yourself through the looking glass of this book. I'm sure it hasn't been easy, and I'm impressed that you have kept reading."

Now you go. Please take the following sentence and write it down. You can send this as a text to the person or read it to them. "I don't know if you know this, but my favorite thing about you is _____ (fill in the blank)."

It can be a meaningful way to thank colleagues or friends, or show admiration for your partner or someone you are interested in. Through this compliment, you can show them what's significant or important to you about them. This can be the safest way to create more intimacy between you and those you care about without oversharing or crossing boundaries. When I say intimacy, I mean safety, security, and genuine connection. I'm not just talking about sex, the honeymoon period, or pursuing someone uninterested in you. Real intimacy is reciprocal and consensual. Healthy intimacy is two (or more) people's capacity to witness and accept one another meaningfully.

How would you feel if someone said this to you? What if someone told you they admire something about you? Would that improve your day? Would it make you feel more appreciated?

What if we did this on a global level? How much more connected would we feel to those around us, including friends and casual contacts? What would happen if we stopped "otherizing" people we are not familiar with, and focused on seeing every person as a valuable being?

If we all did this, how would others treat you differently? If positive words of affirmation were a mainstream phenomenon, how would your life change? Gratitude is the most direct way into others' hearts. Nevertheless, we show very little of it because we are afraid to open our hearts or share what's important to us!

Even if you have experienced trauma around sharing and allowing others to see you, I encourage you to take small steps toward sharing. This practice has been the most liberating part of my personal healing journey. I had withheld myself from relationships for fear of getting hurt. I was afraid I would make a fool of myself or face rejection if I shared my gratitude for others.

Early in life, I learned that no person was safe, which was a lie. When I realized that the abuse I experienced as a child was not what most people encountered, I could permit myself to venture out of my world of fear and into the arms of those who really cared for me. It's from this place of healing that I encourage you to start creating meaningful moments with your loved ones, too. Start with complimenting others, and when you feel ready, learn the art of asking for your needs to be met. Although it may feel scary initially, your courage grows as you practice. You got this!

If you are ready to delve into your needs more deeply but don't know where to start, personality development tools such as Myers-Briggs Type Indicator®, Enneagram, and Human Design can make it easier. Knowing your drives and best-fit types allows you to delve deeper into your needs, and when you realize that there's nothing wrong with you, they may even grant you permission to appreciate and respect yourself on a deeper level. From self-knowledge arises the natural urge to express your needs more compassionately and effectively. These tools can also help you see differences in those around you and how those differences are not good or bad. They just are.

These shared moments of being witnessed - just as you are - build your psycho-emotional stamina to get through your darkest moments with yourself intact. But it's not just helping us face our challenges in life. We can utilize our reservoir of positive self-affirmation to go for what we want and build our dream life one day at a time.

Chapter 24

THE SECRET TO YOUR DREAM LIFE

"The secret to living the life
of your dreams is
to START living the life of your dreams."

- MIKE DOOLEY

As I'M WRITING THE FIRST edit of this book, my ten-year 'Aussieversary' is getting close. "What's Aussieversary," you may ask. It's the anniversary of when I moved to Australia to live the life of my dreams.

While I knew I could not stay in Finland all my life, I never thought my dream life would be on the other side of the world. Yet, I was at the airport, waiting for my partner to pick me up after a twenty-seven-hour journey and emotional goodbyes with my family.

The last time I moved countries, I was twenty. This time around, I was thirty-four and had made sound business and real estate investments to allow me to stop working and just enjoy my dream life. I was in love, free to explore any business or vocational ideas, and living in an off-grid paradise with its own organic fruit and vegetable garden. Soon, we would adopt three horses and two dogs to complete my perfect picture.

*Our off-grid paradise was the ideal safe space I
needed when I moved to Australia.*

You may think, hey, that sounds like a wonderful life. And you are right; it sure was! I meditated for hours for the first six months, ate fresh food, slept, and simply explored my new environment. Then, my mind got bored.

Did I seriously think I could be happy to just chill for the rest of my life? I mean, it's great and all, but if you are a driven individual or a lifelong learner, you know that at some point, the brain has had enough rest, and it's time to take action. I was ready for new dreams to be fulfilled.

For a moment, I didn't know what to do. I had literally never experienced this confusion, and now I was feeling the stress of the unknown. I had always been striving for something and always had goals, ambitions, and dreams. As you can imagine, I felt like I had lost direction in life. It was strange because I was already in a happy, growth-oriented relationship, lived in a paradise, and didn't have to work. You'd think it was perfect, and it was until I got bored and had to create a new dream.

I had already started my self-study when I decided to stop marinating in the self-pity of boredom. I went back to doing bodywork part-time to find some structure for my life. I realized that if I didn't know what to do on a larger scale, I could respond to the opportunities right before me and see where they brought me. I told myself: "just start somewhere and be grateful for what you have."

It turned out that action and gratitude together work wonders. I know this may not be news to you. You may already be a master manifester and think, "Duh, Merja," and I hear you! I was very familiar with the theory but had never applied it in practice, at least not on this scale. I remember attending one of Mike Dooley's workshops in Ireland called Infinite Possibilities. He taught this very method of manifesting the life of your dreams: Visualize, be grateful, and take inspired action. When I looked back at my life, meeting my partner, and moving to Australia, I recognized that I had implemented the theory, just not consciously until now.

My inspired action steps to return to bodywork, as small as they were, helped me integrate into the new country and town and birthed my new career as a personal and business development teacher. Doing part-time bodywork led me to run a donations-only business workshop for local small and medium-sized enterprises. I taught them how I had built my first six-figure business, and how they could do it, too.

I was inspired by the successes my students experienced, and packaged the material into an online course. I even ended up teaching my business success principles at the Start-Up Club in Zurich, Switzerland. As an introvert, it thrilled me to be able to affect change across the world from our little mountainside hideaway.

After having great success with the four-module business workshop, I was ready for more. With the help of some incredible Singleton, New South Wales women, I resurrected the Radiant Woman movement by organizing monthly women's personal empowerment evenings. We playfully called them "the Radiant Women's Wine O'clock meetings."

These meetings turned into further in-person and online courses, which I wrote and facilitated with joy and gratitude in my heart. I achieved all this with the three main activities I learned from Mike: visualize, be grateful, and take inspired action.

Being intentional about what we want from life but appreciating what we already have ignites something powerful within. As Mike says, "Thoughts Become Things." It's like we've been walking around with a blindfold, and with intentional thoughts and actions, our blinkers come off. The same old world turns into a delightful experience of new and abundant opportunities.

Chapter 25

MAKING THE MOST OF YOUR OPPORTUNITIES

"Our mistakes and painful
experiences hold treasure troves
of invaluable knowledge, and this
awareness can illuminate the path
to life's most incredible opportunities."

- LISA WALLACE

ONE OF THESE OPPORTUNITIES CAME my way as I continued my own personal growth. I discovered that I was an introverted, intuitive feeler and judger. "What the heck is that?!" you may ask. It's a reflective, highly intuitive, emotionally aware person who likes order in the outside world.

I always felt like I wasn't "normal". On the one hand, I would decide to move countries because it felt right for me, and on the other, I am one of the most risk-averse people I know. I try to prevent bad things from happening, but if I can't, I deal with any sense of threat head-on, assertively. Effectively, I am both brave and scared, a big dreamer and a practical pragmatist, and, if nothing else, a massive contradiction in terms.

MERJA K. SUMILOFF, LISA WALLACE

This contradiction caused a lot of confusion in my life, which I never understood until I discovered my personality type. As I read my personality type assessment results on my computer screen, I whispered to myself: "I am an INFJ. I am an introverted, intuitive feeler, and judger. A deeply feeling person with high-level pattern-recognition skills and a tender heart. I tend to dream big and want to make order and decisions in the outside world".

"FAAAAAR OUT!" I blurted out. This Australian saying that expresses astonishment had already become a near-everyday saying for me. Now, it all made sense. With the guidance of my heart, I had made all my life's crucial decisions based on the vivid picture of what I wanted. My heart told me where to move, and once the decision was made, I filled in the grid of practicalities with meticulous details through a well-thought-out plan.

Being prepared ensured that I always created a safe space ahead of my arrival, be it creatively, physically, or financially. Could I have done better with my decisions? Sure, although I don't regret any of my choices. Knowing that pain has a purpose and is an influential teacher helped me make the most of any "bad" decisions. The past mistakes have given me plenty of opportunities to learn and fail forward.

With the "diagnosis of having a condition called INFJ," I took a deep dive into the Myers-Briggs Type Indicator® system. Each of the sixteen types under this system described people I knew in my life. With my blooming interest in personal development came more questions. My brain had been kicked back into gear after the initial rest, and I was raring to go. Studying my type gave me a sense of relief. This personality typing system was the nurturing I needed to bring my intellect to life. Finally, there was a logical explanation for my weirdness, and I could stop apologizing for being me.

When you discover and accept who you are,
you can rest into your talents fully.

[Note from the authors: You can check out the sixteen type overviews from the official Myers-Briggs Type Indicator® page www.myersbriggs.org/my-mbti-personality-type/mbti-basics/, or get in touch with the Sumiloff Academy - sumiloff.com - if you are curious about your own type, and how to heal, develop, and master your life through it.]

My mind could not get enough of the theory. My intuition started seeing patterns everywhere, but now I saw them more clearly. I realized that in my immature years, I had misinterpreted people and situations. With this new knowledge of my natural wiring, I learned that many of my past relationship dynamics were based on my trauma and not who I really was underneath it!

I'm not afraid to admit that I had assigned false meaning to circumstances in my life and projected my insecurities onto others' behavior. For example, whenever anyone around me was angry, I automatically asserted that the situation was dangerous. As I matured and discovered my natural wiring, I realized that sometimes people are just mad and that it has nothing to do with me. I can't tell you how freeing that realization was for me.

While I'd come across and studied the Enneagram system in my twenties, discovering my MBTI® personality type felt like hitting the jackpot. Using these two systems in my own personal development gave me what felt like a detailed and practical self-operating manual. The deeper I got into my personality profile, the more at home I felt. This discovery of a "home within" encouraged me to share this newfound sense of inner safety with others through my work. To this day, I help my students create their own personal operations manual for healing, developing, and mastering their lives.

The first pure personal development course I wrote was a love letter to my own type, INFJ, and what I call the sibling type, INFP (Introverted iNtuitive Feeling Perceivers). While their cognitive functions differ, these two types have eerily similar life experiences. I discovered that many of the most beloved people in my life were either INFJs or INFPs and as I wrote, I made sure to jot down all the things we wished someone had taught us lovingly in our youth. I called the course INFx Unveiled, because it worked across both INF types, and helped these incredible individuals discover and share themselves with the world in a more authentic way.

Most of the world is not geared toward highly intuitive or feeling individuals. These gifts are often overlooked and even categorized as unimportant. This course filled the hearts of thousands of introverted intuitive feelers worldwide because, for the very first time, they felt seen. My students dubbed the INFx Unveiled "the best and most validating program" they had ever encountered. It made them feel profoundly understood and appreciated.

The course acted as a secret nod to the challenges we had experienced most of our lives. Within three months of the launch of this program, Personality Hacker, a famous personality development website and podcast, published it. I was thrilled and grateful that my love letter for these incredible but marginalized people would reach an even wider audience.

Spurred on by my personality type and the success of the INFx Unveiled, I wrote another eleven personal and professional development courses over the next nine years. As with writing this book, I have always felt at my most satisfied when putting pen to paper. I know I'm not alone in this feeling. Many other introverts know what I'm talking about, particularly intuitive feelers. It's easier to put our complex thoughts in writing than it is to communicate them verbally.

As the course became widely spread, I received hundreds of messages of appreciation because those who took it finally felt seen for who they were. I also gave them a safe space to work through their innermost challenges. The feedback I received was speaking straight to my heart. It touched me deeply because with my INFJ "diagnosis," I finally felt at home within myself, and now others could too.

Most of the positive feedback came from those who, like me, had experienced a turbulent childhood. My course taught them how to build a container of nurturing calm within themselves. I had succeeded with my intent. I wanted every person on the planet to experience having a safe space for themselves where they could self-actualize and heal.

My dream life expanded around me as my influence grew and I developed. I made the most of my opportunities by formalizing my personality development training and achieving the Myers-Briggs Type Indicator® professional certification. The more authentically I lived from my tender heart, the wider the healing impact of my work. As Mike Dooley had predicted, the secret to my dream life was to start living it and sharing it with others in a meaningful and caring way.

Chapter 26

OPINIONS THAT MATTER

"All opinions are not created equal."

- MERJA SUMILOFF

EVERYONE HAS AN OPINION, AND they are entitled to it. But just because someone has an opinion doesn't automatically mean the opinion is relevant. Let's assume that we have moved beyond thinking that there is only one ultimate truth and we agree that most people see things a little differently. The differences in perspectives are formed by our cognitive capacities, values, and lived experience, so it's easy to see that there cannot be one ultimate truth when it comes to life.

I see opinions as vocalized expressions of our cognition, values, and lived experience thus far. But I believe that our opinions also expose our hopes, fears, and insecurities. Effectively, if we pay close enough attention to all opinions, we get an insight into the person's subjective outlook in life. Bill Pollard famously said that an opinion is the lowest form of knowledge because it doesn't require any accountability or understanding. I agree. Just because you, I, or Joe Bloggs up the road has an opinion, it doesn't automatically mean that the opinion is relevant or even valuable for someone else.

If we want to hold our focus and live intentionally, we must learn to discern between opinions that are relevant to us and those that are not. To see if an opinion is relevant, we can measure the applicability of the opinion. If the opinion is not applicable, it is just background noise that distracts us from building our meaningful life. Don't forget that we all get to assess others' opinions, and we, the recipients, get to give those opinions the weight and meaning they deserve.

So, what happens when others have an opinion about you or your work and share it without being asked? What should we do when we receive this kind of unsolicited feedback?

If you're anything like me, I immediately take others' opinions to heart and attempt to take action to correct the situation swiftly. After writing the INFx Unveiled course using the Myers-Briggs Type Indicator® personality inventory, a person on Reddit called me stupid for thinking that my approach could help anyone. They said I could not write a course for INFJs and INFPs because these two types don't share any cognitive functionalities. At first, I felt taken aback. Because of my childhood abuse and the constant gaslighting, I immediately thought their criticism was valid and that I should apologize and fix the problem.

But as I calmed down, I realized I had not asked for their opinion. This was literally the opinion of a person who had not even taken the course. This person had wholly overlooked the shared real-life experiences that INFJs and INFPs face daily. The course was not as much about the technical functioning of the types as it was about giving comfort and support to people who had not experienced a safe space growing up.

If you are an introverted intuitive feeler, you know how it feels when the sensory-thinking world marginalizes our perspectives and strengths. Thanks to many emotionally mature industry leaders, intuition and feeling are now being recognized as assets, not just liabilities. But, much like any other phenomenon of marginalization, the insidious hangover of "how things should be" and "what is appropriate" can take time to change. Just because people recognize the importance of intuition and compassion does not mean these cognitive strengths have become mainstream. Yet.

I see the same hangover in the world of equestrianism as well. Too much emphasis on tradition stands in the way of the inevitable progress as we discover horses more deeply as sentient beings. I've seen the same ignorant comments attacking some of our most treasured teachers of a more natural approach to horsemanship. It's the same toxic ego attached to its knowledge: anything that is different must be wrong.

It's said that unsolicited advice is always criticism. I agree with this sentiment. I also know that everyone has the right to speak their truth, which means that if you put yourself in the public eye, you will be given unsolicited advice. In other words, you will be criticized.

So, I decided to turn the tables on the critics I encountered. I noted their uneducated opinions about my work and printed them out. There were four paragraphs in total. I then printed out fourteen pages of success stories from people my work had helped. I compared the two and realized that what mattered was the results of those who took the time to study and work through the material. The benefits of my work clearly outweigh the criticism. That was all I needed to know to let go of someone's hurtful opinion of my "stupidity disguised as knowledge."

Another time I came across criticism, it hit closer to home. After writing the INFx Unveiled course, I wrote the 4 People Within® program. The Sumiloff Academy mentors-in-training use a part of the program to help their case study clients discover who they are and how they make decisions. At the end of the nine complimentary sessions with student mentors, I conduct a feedback call with each case study client. Even though I was inviting criticism to help us grow, one case study client hit me with: "The 4 People Within® theory is such a dyslexic mess. Clearly, whoever wrote it is not very coherent."

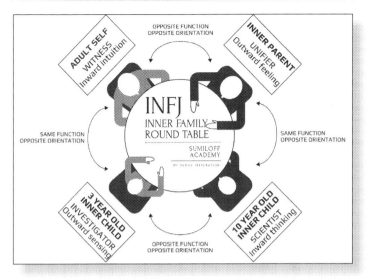

My 4 People Within® round table diagram for Introverted iNtuitive Feeler Judger [Graphic work by the amazing Sanna Kontiola]

As a dyslexic person, her words hurt my feelings. But as a seasoned professional, I parked my hurt and became curious. I asked the case study client about the wins they had experienced throughout their work with the student mentor. They listed several victories, including getting through a nasty breakup of a long-term relationship. I then asked if they could determine when they made vital decisions with their head versus their heart, and they said yes. Despite the confusion this client had experienced around the concept, they had learned to utilize the 4 People Within® for better decision-making.

I was gobsmacked. Why would this person criticize me and my work if they had benefited from it directly and in a relatively short period of time? It made no sense to me. Digging into it further, I realized that the student mentor had not pointed out the connection between the theory and the results the client was experiencing. I thought: "Isn't that interesting?". One sentence clearly relayed and understood could have clarified the value of my work to the client.

I thanked the case study client for the call and took their feedback seriously without taking it personally. I reviewed the learning material to see if there was something I could improve on. In the end, I was happy with the material as it was, and reminded myself that just because someone has an opinion doesn't mean it warrants action from me. Maybe the problem wasn't even the material. Perhaps the client wasn't open to studying theory for whatever reason. Nevertheless, that conversation gave *me* an opportunity to become a clearer communicator without discounting the value of my work.

This lesson has served me well. This case study client reminded me about the importance of clear and concise communication. This one encounter alone has made all the difference for our Academy Ambassadors out there in the world as they share our message of hope, healing, and personal power.

Chapter 27

CONSENT BEFORE AN OPINION

"Consent opens the door for
the insight to be received."

- MERJA SUMILOFF

*W*HEN I REFLECTED ON OTHERS' opinions about who I am and what I do, I started playing around with the concept of consent before an opinion. This fundamental premise of asking for permission before sharing our opinions began taking shape. When someone doesn't ask for your permission to share their observations, you don't have to consent and listen to what they say. This also works in reverse. When you don't ask for permission to share your opinions with others, they are under no obligation to take on what you have to say. No matter how valuable your opinion may be, if the person is not asking for it, they are unlikely to hear and benefit from it.

Failing to hear answers to questions we haven't asked is a basic human condition. We shift and sort through information coming at us according to our interests and need to know. It's also worth noting that in a world full of critics, consciously ignoring the unwanted opinions that may erode our self-esteem and productivity is a critical life skill.

My experiences in the public eye have forced me to come up with my personal procedure around unsolicited advice. It reads:

1. If I don't know and trust you, I won't be open to hearing your opinion. For too long, my abusive conditioning led to accepting all feedback as facts. This led me into further unkind relationships and situations. To protect me from any potential manipulation, I want to ensure that I can trust you to have my best interest at heart.

2. If you don't respect me, I probably won't take on your opinion. Why would I? Your opinion is most likely coming from the same source as your attitude toward me: disrespect.

3. If you haven't produced what you criticize me for, I don't need to hear your "advice." Many who have never started a business attempt to advise those facing business challenges. Why? If you don't have first-hand experience with the challenge I'm going through, your criticism will likely be unhelpful.

If you are in the process of finding your inner strength, you may have to protect your dignity by refusing opinions that didn't come with consent. For this stage of personal empowerment, many adopt the following statement: "If you haven't asked permission to share your observations, I am not open to hearing them."

If you have experienced personal violation and marginalization, you may not have developed a strong core sense of self. This makes standing up for yourself difficult. Listening to others' subjective opinions about your situation may sway you from your authentic life path. Learning to set boundaries with others' unsolicited advice is a fundamental skill for continued self-establishment.

If your childhood has permanently scarred your sense of self, you may have to work harder to stop unwanted influences on your life. Everyone's intent is not malicious. However, the predatory people out there have - what seems like - a sixth sense for identifying people who lack healthy boundaries.

Studies show that pathological abusers know what to look for in their victims. They look for your posture, confidence of gait, and unhealthy situational awareness. When predators sense damage to your self-esteem, they try to exploit you.

The problem is that low self-esteem often originates from past abusive experiences. If you know someone who has experienced abuse, you may have noticed that they don't carry themselves with the same confidence as before their attack. Thus, abuse leads to low self-esteem, which in turn can lead to more abuse. This phenomenon explains why it can be hard to leave abusive situations and why the abused seem to repeat their past mistakes.

But not all abuse is predatory or pathological. An innocent misunderstanding in an everyday relationship may be experienced as abusive. When our relationships lack the concept of consent, our cognitive capacity, values, and lived experience can leave us feeling abused by a well-meaning other.

I remember witnessing an exchange between an ex-partner and his mother. When this ex suggested that he pick his mother up from church because her car was in the shop being fixed, her natural response to his offering was, "Don't be stupid! I can walk". While she intended not to make a nuisance of herself, her messaging was abusive to a man whose father had told him repeatedly as a child that he was stupid. You can see how a careless or poorly timed sentence meant to comfort another can feel abusive if we fail to check in with them first.

Being present and asking for permission to share one's opinion is a sign of good manners and a way to protect others' integrity and dignity. My ex's mother could have simply said, "Thank you for offering, but I will walk home." It's good to remember that our good intentions don't always translate well into our spoken language. Being present and mindful of how we speak to others is important, especially when we inevitably have to have hard conversations about health, expectations, and hurts.

Consent extends grace to our interactions, especially when it comes to sharing our opinions. But sometimes consent is not enough! I like to pre-qualify my opinion by asking questions. When someone comes to me in pain asking for help, I don't simply start spraying them with the streams of my intuitive interpretations. I want to make sure that my opinions are relevant to their situation. A simple question: "What kind of support would be helpful for you right now?" embraces consent while preserving the sovereignty of the person struggling.

Similarly, if you are struggling yourself, set boundaries with others' attempts to "help" you. Choose to seek advice from people you trust and respect and who ask questions before sharing their opinions. Has the person experienced the struggle you are going through? Would they be willing to share their golden nuggets of knowledge with you? If you want to empower yourself, I encourage you to have practical conversations with those who have overcome your current struggles. I also advocate that you only work with those who communicate in a supportive and respectful manner to protect your dignity.

If you're a survivor of abuse like me, I want to embolden you to reject opinions that don't preserve your sense of self, and are designed to keep you playing small. A keyboard warrior's opinion about me cannot matter because I have bigger plans. I can't get sidetracked by someone's opinion, especially if they didn't ask for consent or their opinion is not relevant or applicable. My focus is on my fifty-year commitment to creating a more joyous, compassionate, creative, and effective world for us and future generations. Setting loving boundaries with myself to know which feedback to listen to is an integral part of this process.

What about you? What is your focus in life? What do you want to be remembered for? What will you do next time someone gives you an uninformed or uninvited opinion disguised as helpful advice?

Staking a claim in life is scary. It may leave us open to criticism from others, who may or may not understand what we are trying to achieve. But be brave, my friend. If you want to see a difference in the world:

1. Be part of it.
2. Make it happen.
3. Don't be distracted by the wrenches of ignorance others throw into your works.

Life is hard enough as it is, especially if you have experienced trauma and have a yearning to heal from it. Many of your internal challenges are already taking so much of your focus. So let others have their opinions, and you focus on nurturing your most precious asset: **YOU**.

Study on predators - https://www.researchgate.net/publication/235669299_Psychopathy_and_Victim_Selection_The_Use_of_Gait_as_a_Cue_to_Vulnerability

Part IV

THE DEEP WELL

Chapter 28

TRIGGERED

*T*RIGGER WARNING: IF YOU OR your loved one is struggling with thoughts or acts of suicide, PTS, PTSD, or C-PTSD, what I have written here may activate your stress response. If it does, please stop reading now and get help from a local mental health practitioner. Please remember that this is my story and not necessarily a reflection of what you or your loved one is going through.

With love, Merja.

> "Unless you learn to face
> your own shadows,
> you will continue to see them in others
> because the world outside you is
> only a reflection of the world inside you."
>
> - CARL JUNG

According to the Mayo Clinic, the seven symptoms of Post-traumatic stress disorder (PTSD) are:

- Easily startled or frightened
- On guard for danger at all times

- Self-destructive behavior, such as drinking too much or driving too fast
- Trouble sleeping
- Difficulty concentrating
- Irritability, angry outbursts, or aggressive behavior
- Overwhelming guilt or shame

I was sitting in the cupboard of the recording studio, shaking. I didn't know what was happening, but I knew it was unsafe to come out. Before barricading into the cupboard, I had locked the doors, checked the windows, and switched the lights off. The door-locking, I understood. While I didn't know why my instinct was to switch the lights off, somehow, there was comfort in the darkness.

It was late at night, the sun had set, and I had just finished recording the day's last 4 People Within® course modules. If you've ever had to make recordings of what you have written, you know how challenging it can be to read your work aloud. On top of that, I was in double trouble: to the left of me were my challenges with dyslexia while reading out loud, and from the right, I could feel my PTSD flanking me.

It was a long recording session: there were thirteen pages to read, which might as well have been a three hundred thousand-word book for someone living with dyslexia. But I had psyched myself up for this session because it was no ordinary one. The topic of the day's last recording was PTSD.

Throughout the recording, I was fumbling around with my reading and speaking, not simply because of dyslexia. I couldn't breathe properly. The growing metallic smell of the inevitable post-traumatic trigger was thick in the air, as it always was when it was too late to turn back. I felt suffocated well before the trigger snapped. I was having severe difficulty getting the words out of my mouth and onto the voice file, so I knew what was coming.

With every word I spoke, the traumatic memories came back. After realizing my family's mental health issues in my twenties, I went to therapy. Therapy had helped me settle into the knowledge of my trauma, and I had thought that I was done with my healing just by understanding trauma.

Over a decade later, sitting in the cupboard, I realized that no amount of theoretical knowledge would help me complete my healing process. I was triggered by reading the words describing one of my original traumas. The tentacles of the darkness wrapped around my neck, and they were pulling me down.

In my mind, I was back in that house, being chased by those two men. As clear as day was the reality of hiding between the boxes of potatoes, waiting to be found and brutalized. My mind was repeating the events on a loop, and any time the threat passed, my thoughts would jump back into waking up in the bed upstairs, overhearing them talk about what they would do to me.

The situation and the studio environment were a perfect storm. While working, I revisited my old trauma, even if just in my mind. The surroundings emulated my childhood terror: I felt alone in a strange house with unfamiliar noises. It was dark outside, just like it had been in that house of horrors.

It makes complete sense that I had been triggered. Both my trauma and the day of the recording included the same ingredients. Yet, I felt powerless to do anything about it. Just like that, I was back to being that five-year-old child with no one protecting her. The fear felt like a stormy sea, and the darkness of the abuse kept pulling me underwater. Instinctually, I knew that if the story cycle kept twirling around in my mind, I would lose myself, maybe forever.

Thankfully, I had already worked with my painful past and knew about the dark forest. I knew I was safe as long as I could keep the flashlight of my focus on visiting the forest and not getting lost there. So I faced the forest, knowing that as long as the lantern of my inner light had enough fuel, I could find my way in and out again.

Thank goodness I had gone through this before and had gotten help. Over the years, I had become aware and present with my triggering. Early on in life, I realized that fighting my PTS alone would not work, nor pretending it wasn't there. The only approach that worked consistently was to share my experiences with others and respect the post-traumatic stress as a visitor from the past instead of identifying with it. Recovery requires the unapologetic ownership of my trauma and the stress that follows the triggers. There is no space for shame in recovery, although overcoming it can be one of the most challenging parts of healing.

I had to be strong in the lead-up to, and full-on moments of triggering. I had to fight the temptation to surrender to the familiarity of the shadows of my trauma. I would be okay if I could remember that *I was a person and not my trauma*. If I allowed myself to identify with the trauma and think that that's all I am, I would drown in the dark waters of my past pain.

As a reflex and almost as a prediction of my inevitable travel to the dark forest, I had switched off the recording room's lights. My body and actions played out the old trauma as I hid in the darkness just as I had done thirty-five years earlier. None of it made sense to the intellect, but the body truly keeps the score.

If you've experienced trauma, you understand that it (trauma) is what it is **until you are ready to shape it into something else**. Healing the past pain, releasing it from your cells, and transforming it into something positive takes time. Trauma is a shape-shifter that needs loving boundaries so that it can be transformed into an inner sense of power. Victims become powerful creators only when they learn to use the tools necessary and take the time to find the power beyond their trauma. Seeing yourself in this new way may take time, but you're not the only one affected.

When my students undergo this transformation, I remind them that they are becoming a whole new person. Effectively, they are changing the relationship dynamics others are used to. This maneuver solicits a range of reactions from those who are already in their lives. I tell my students: "Some people who are already in your life will want you to keep playing small. They are highly invested in you staying the same, so you are likely to ruffle some feathers. But those who love you for who you are, want you to be happy, and may even be inspired to grow with you."

I tell my students to expect attacks, manipulation, and even bribery from those who want them to stay the same. I tell them: "This is the time you must stay strong and stay true to yourself." When my students transform their pain into power, their situational awareness improves, they begin to call people out on bad behavior, and their posture and gait become more assured. The perpetrators and the enablers notice this and disappear because they sense that these students are no longer vulnerable to their attacks.

It can be hard to hold your ground when you have discovered a truth within you that changes the dynamics of your existing relationships. Remember to fail forward. You, too, are learning! It takes time, practice, and dedication to your truth to keep going. Although I know all this, when triggered, my mind, too, goes blank. It's like I'm a beginner again! That day, all I could do was to follow my instinct to hide.

In many ways, the relative size of the cupboard reminded me of the gap between the boxes of potatoes. The tablecloths in the closet were the perfect replacement for the hessian bags I'd hidden under as a child. So I pulled them over me and hid to feel safe. Even though I was on the other side of the world, it felt like I had traveled back in time. There were thirty-five years between the childhood injury and that moment. I was an adult with security measures in place. I was living in safety, yet the past still had this grip on me as it terrorized me into hiding.

For those that have not experienced PTS, I'm so glad for you. You may think: "s-e-r-i-o-u-s-l-y; you're a grown-ass woman, a thought leader, and an author recording a course audio, literally a two-minute drive from home. You are a deliberate creator! What's wrong with you?".

I understand. I had manifested my dream life in a safe location, and my partner was just a call away if I needed help. But none of that mattered at that moment. My experience was not anchored in the current reality. It was fixed in the past, and that was my reality. It didn't matter that I was safe; I didn't *feel* safe. It didn't even cross my mind that my partner could come to help me because, in my reality, I was five and left to fend for myself.

Source: https://www.mayoclinic.org/diseases-conditions/post-traumatic-stress-disorder/symptoms-causes/syc-20355967

Chapter 29

EMPOWERMENT THROUGH PTSD

> "Trauma is not what happens to you:
> trauma is what happens inside you
> as a result of what happens to you."
>
> - GABOR MATE

Recording the PTSD module was the perfect storm. But it was also a self-induced triggering. I had not mindfully planned around my potential post-traumatic triggering. I had chosen to speak about my trauma without having a safe person with me. I'd even left my trusted service dog, Clifford, at home because I didn't want to inconvenience the studio owners. Through a series of self-marginalizing micro-decisions, I had helped create my triggering.

It's not unusual for abused children to grow up to become self-sacrificing adults. That's certainly what happened to me. But most abused children also don't learn how to speak up. My childhood conditioning taught me to keep my mouth shut. The house of horrors had been a close call. But the times I didn't escape, the abusers told me no one would believe me, and the enablers told me not to shame the family with my "lies."

As if the trauma wasn't enough. Throughout my life, I also had to deal with not being believed. When my aunt told me that all these bad things were just in my imagination, I thought, "Umm...

no. I don't just have a colorful imagination. I have trauma, and you are attempting to gaslight me because you either don't know or don't want to find out."

In the studio, my recorded words had activated my trauma because I had chosen to speak up. If I recorded my story, thousands of people would witness it. What if they, too, would attempt to marginalize my pain and gaslight me?

I had been okay writing the module. But while recording it, I was changing the paradigm. I was expressing my truth verbally - something I had never been able to do as a child. While reading the words was hard, that wasn't the trigger. The trigger for my PTS episode was expecting the abuse that followed from speaking out.

No one made me do this. I didn't have to write or record the course; I had chosen to do it to help others heal. I had decided to take action to empower myself, and it was possible that I would get hurt in the process. Many victims refuse to speak up or do the healing work for this exact reason. Intuitively, they know that before they are empowered, the perpetrators and their enablers will attack them again. I was getting a post-traumatic response because I knew what was coming. But it wasn't someone else that had put me into this compromised situation. I could not blame anyone else when, inevitably, I would be attacked. In this instance, the boogie man was me.

Tiina's words rang in my ears: "If you are the common denominator, you also have the power to change the narrative." The PTS had completely changed my perception of myself. This type of injury makes you forget who you are. It throws you into the depths of your most vulnerable state. If you have never experienced PTS, it's probably hard to understand how a person can flip from being themselves into an alternative reality within a split second.

But in my experience, we can slip into our stress response over time, or instantaneously. I have experienced every variation of triggering and learned to recover from it. The common denominator for our recovery is not the time it takes to bounce back. It is how skilled and resilient we are in managing our trigger and moving past the ordeal.

If we only focus on our trauma and allow it to define us, we begin to wire our brains to think we are always in danger. When untreated, the trauma creates solid neural pathways in our brains and stores toxic memories within our cells. Next, it enrolls the hippocampus to create a reel for our life that plays the story of us as a victim on an endless loop. That's what had happened to me in the cupboard. My thoughts had gone on in an endless loop with no perceivable way out. Outwardly, we may seem completely normal, but our cells are hard-wired for hyper-vigilance.

If we are lucky, we know that we live in two realities: the trauma reality and the non-trauma, current reality. But if we are not aware of the effects of past trauma, it can trick us into believing that we are still in imminent danger. Our whole world can feel fractured and ever-changing, as if we were watching life through a kaleidoscope. No matter what perspective we try to take, the pieces simply don't fit. People who live with unhealed trauma may live their whole lives in a state of hyper-vigilance, making sure to keep one eye on what could go wrong at all times. They don't see a safe space, even if one is presented to them.

Trauma, shame, guilt - and yes, PTSD - are like mushrooms. They grow and expand in the darkness. If we want to overcome our PTS and live a more calm and enjoyable life, we must learn how to ask for help and share our experiences with those we trust and respect. Meaningful connections with others bring about psycho-emotional resilience. When we learn to communicate our challenges with those significant others, we can feel witnessed in our struggle. When others have a clear picture of what we are going through, they are more able to meet us and offer us a safe space where we can finally heal.

Before I started sharing my experience with trusted others, I felt exhausted because I existed within two separate worlds. I was bouncing between the trauma reality and the non-trauma reality, depending on the stimulus from my surroundings. If I felt safe, I could relax and enjoy my life. If I was in a new or stressful situation, the hyper-vigilance showed up with its well-meaning but debilitating focus on every possible detail.

From moment to moment, I had to choose which world I lived and participated in. I had to restrict the amount of new information I would take in and schedule rest time after new or stressful experiences. If I didn't, my cellular memory attempted to absorb the brewing storm of terror within me. If I pushed myself too far, my physical frame would shake in anticipation of a trigger. If I didn't stay present with my body, it was just a matter of time before I would explode.

I didn't suffer from PTSD for decades because I was so traumatized. For sure, the abuse itself traumatized me. My PTSD originated from my inability to reconcile the abuse I'd suffered. I had trouble making sense of the abuse because I genuinely thought I had caused it and deserved it. My father repeatedly told me that I was the reason his life was ruined and others were unhappy. On some level, I had accepted this as a fact, even though it couldn't possibly be true.

But what happened was not my fault. I had done nothing to deserve the abuse. **I was just a child, and my abuse was simply the effect of other traumatized people passing on their pain instead of working to face it.** I struggled for decades because I thought it was my fault and was afraid to ask for help. Until I dared to speak up, I kept picking up the tab for others' ignored pain.

But everything changed for me when I learned to talk about what happened, how it affected me, and ask for help. Talking helped, as it shed light on the dark corners of my insecurities. I learned that I had been laboring under some wrong assumptions:

1. I thought that I was responsible for others' emotions, and
2. I had to keep an eye on everything in order to see where the next attack was coming from.

But if you've ever tried to micromanage the world around you, you know how impossible and unsustainable it is. I could relax when I realized that I was only responsible for *my* feelings and actions. Learning what personal responsibilities are helped me understand that I didn't have to keep waiting for bad things to happen to me, and that I was allowed to build a life that wasn't just about survival.

I also learned to use my post-traumatic stress reactions as signposts for healing and personal development. Whenever I bumped up against a trigger, I asked myself: **what lie or misplaced expectation had I accepted as a fact concerning this issue?** In no time, I would realize other toxic childhood messages I had absorbed as facts. With this clarity, I knew what I needed to work on next and rolled up my sleeves.

This meticulous approach to healing and personal development led to excellent relationships with myself and others. When healed and transformed, my triggering helped me create a deep, compassionate, and loving relationship with my life and its important people.

Taking the trauma narrative and deliberately flipping it into empowerment gave me an entirely new perspective on life. For the longest time, I thought I would be defined by the abuse and trauma I had experienced as a child. But I was wrong. As I healed, I realized that I could turn my father's legacy of pain into an inheritance of knowledge, creativity, and personal power.

Chapter 30

THE LEGACY OF MY TRAUMA

"Trauma, if harnessed, can
power your ambition."

- MERJA SUMILOFF

As I SOBERED UP FROM the cocktail of stress hormones and my psyche returned to the recording room, I put the tablecloths aside, opened the cupboard doors, and stood up. Everything felt different from that moment on. I haven't visited a cupboard since that day of recording. Not to protect myself from triggers or because I'm hiding in other ways. I have stood strong with my chin up because after recovering from the studio incident, I decided to face the surfacing terrors head-on.

Relying on Tiina's words and following the string back to the shore, I decided to put my psycho-emotional baggage down. I looked around for the first time without the terror of hyper-vigilance. Where I had heard a threat before, I now saw possums making noise. Where I had seen a threatening darkness, I saw a natural end of the day. Setting down my baggage and owning my experience, I became vividly aware of myself in the universal flow of life and energy. I felt reborn.

I packed up and went home with this new awareness. I debriefed my partner about what had happened and felt reassured by his arms around me. I wept as I released the psycho-emotional terror that the little girl within me had carried for decades.

This was the first time in my conscious experience that I felt witnessed and not judged. I'm sure others had offered that to me before, but I simply could not see or feel it. That moment forged my knowing that I no longer had to hide to feel safe. I had discovered another level of safety within myself and with those I trust and love.

The cellular memory release was palpable. My body found a freedom I had not felt before. My tinnitus was gone, and my back felt strong and supple for the first time in years. As the shape of my trauma had changed from a hidden secret to a shared moment of intimacy, my life opened up in a whole new way. In that one moment of embrace with my partner, I could feel my consciousness expand beyond anything I had felt before.

My beloved partner Peter and I

As I slumbered that night, the waves of my subconscious mind pushed a bottle to the beach of my consciousness. In my dream, I picked up the bottle, hesitant from the conditioned defensiveness I had lived with most of my life. I pulled out the cork with a pop and carefully pulled out an old piece of paper. I could feel my heart pounding in my chest like it does when I'm about to receive a message or a significant insight from the universe.

The message was: "Don't let the trauma fool you into thinking it's ONLY a bad thing."

I remember waking up at night to this message, confused. For as long as I can remember, we labeled trauma as "bad," and anyone who didn't have a safe childhood or life experience was always "trying to heal so they could become a normal, functioning person." But what if experiencing my trauma wasn't just a "bad" thing? What if it didn't disqualify me from having a joyous, compassionate, creative, and effective life?

My thoughts raced as this new paradigm took shape in my mind. Shifting my focus from "all trauma is bad, all of the time" to "my trauma has a purpose and a legacy" solidified my perspective as a powerful creator. I want to take this opportunity to reiterate that I am NOT in favor of spiritual bypasses. I hope it's clear by now that I am an unyielding advocate for mental health and healing. What I am saying is that for me at that time, I was ready to become an alchemist and make gold out of my painful past. Then, I fell back asleep.

The following day, I faintly remembered the new message of power. It felt like the scent of a perfume from the night before: it had seeped into my skin and was now a part of me until I had cleansed myself of it. Only I didn't want to be cleansed of this sense of power. The shift felt instinctively profound and intuitively healing. But I didn't want to just run with it! Too often, I had gotten excited about a possibility only to find myself on the wrong track. I wanted to double-check my new perception with the most accurate barometer of instinct I knew: my horses.

If you know horses, you know how perceptive they are. They can tell when you are energetically aligned with yourself because they are relaxed and accepting around you. If you are not in alignment, your horses sense that and become tense. Horses know when you are pushing through life and when you are relaxed in the flow of it. In my experience, if I'm not aligned with myself, my horses either stay away from me or feel the need to take over as leaders. It's like they can tap into my emotional landscape and say: "I don't want to have anything to do with you today," or "You're not safe to lead our herd today. You are too emotional, and I must take over."

In the morning light, I had a drink of water and walked down into the paddock. I sat down where the horses could see me but didn't approach them. It was a windy day, and I knew that if I had relaxed into the universal flow of life, my horses would come to me, relaxed, despite the wind. I also knew that if I were attempting a spiritual bypass, my internal misalignment would repel them.

In unison, they looked up, and one after another, they walked over. They sniffed me as if to say: "Hello. Nice to meet you, new Merja." I burst into tears, and they stood over me as I sobbed. Although I was emotional, I was grounded. My horses saw past the emotion and recognized that I was solid in my truth. Their "blessing" was a sacred moment. It also confirmed to me that I was on the right path to understanding the real legacy of my trauma.

Some may say this is an anthropomorphic projection to make meaning from nothing. Others may think I'm looking for biased confirmation of my made-up story. They may be right. But I also knew that once I started acting on this message in the bottle, the sensory world around me would show me if I was wrong. I knew from past experience, that if I was on the wrong track, life would become increasingly challenging and impractical.

I felt that I had stepped away from my painful past and into a new reality of freedom. I took a moment to thank my horses and enjoy basking in the glory of their deeply instinctive knowledge. Much like my experience with Donut nearly four decades before, I felt assured, free, and sovereign. I was ready to step into this new paradigm.

I've found that when we follow an authentic insight, we begin to see doors we didn't even know existed. Before the insight, you might feel completely isolated and lonely. You may feel like no one cares about or understands you. You may also think that others are too busy, and you don't want to bother them with your struggles. But then, you have an insight, and it's as if the world as a whole adjusts to your new reality. As long as you stay true to your insight and take thoughtful action aligned with it, an unexplored world keeps unfolding around you.

The first thing that changed for me was my relationships. Outside my significant and close family relationships, I had felt disempowered. For years, I had tried to navigate the challenging line between my genuine care for my students and being too familiar and friendly with them.

I realized that many of my friendships were simply free mentoring, and for the first time, I admitted that I felt used. Many "friends" never asked how I was during a two-hour phone conversation about their latest drama. My new insight showed that this dynamic had to change.

It was interesting to observe that when I let go of my non-reciprocal friendships, the people who really loved and cared for me would step forward. Setting boundaries around how I wanted to be loved and respected brought about that exact experience. I couldn't believe it. When I stopped being the victim, others stopped victimizing me.

I took this intent to my work, too. When I let go of students who pushed my boundaries, I attracted incredibly thoughtful ones who valued me and were excited to join me in building the vision of a more joyous, compassionate, creative, and effective world. My work life went from trying to rescue others to becoming a highly paid, productive, and appreciated guide for life-long learners who were ready to heal and transform.

The more empowered I felt within myself, the more authentically compassionate and effective I was able to be with my students. Remembering my worth and power helped me remind them of theirs. I had stopped seeing myself and others *as the trauma we had experienced* and started treating everyone with more dignity and care.

Encouraged by my personal and work results, I began sharing my experiences more openly. Having been an intensely private person, I decided to open up in the service of others. That's how this book came about.

How many other people were struggling alone like I had? Who else needs to hear that their trauma is not all of who they are? Who needed to hear my story of quiet defiance? Having shared my experiences earnestly and vulnerably, my soul broke open for even more positive change. Having a sense of true clarity, healing, love, and belonging, I could no longer justify playing small. The true legacy of my trauma was *in healing it and sharing my knowledge to empower others.*

The puck of pain had stopped here.

Chapter 31

PASSING ON YOUR POWERFUL LEARNINGS

> "We gain sacred wisdom and empower ourselves during life's most significant challenges and adversities. We serve others by passing on our insightful golden nuggets to them."
>
> - LISA WALLACE

I WILL NEVER FORGET THE CALL. The brave woman's voice shook as she told me what had unfolded over the last few days. Her husband of fourteen years was not who she thought he was. He wasn't just the father of her children and her abusive life partner. She had discovered that he was also a drug dealer and an addict. His habit had landed him deeply in debt to the wrong people. If he didn't pay what he owed, the suppliers would hurt her and her children.

Needless to say, the woman was in shock and danger. She was in pain and disbelief. She had been deeply betrayed, and although I knew I could help her, attempting to coach her to shift her perspective from a victim to a powerful creator at that moment was completely inappropriate.

As I was listening to her speak, my mind kicked into gear. What does she *actually* need right now? I realized that the threat to her life was no longer only domestic. Her narrative had changed from "it's not safe in the house" to "it's not safe anywhere."

I thanked her for telling me what was going on. I said I had some questions and checked that it was okay to ask. She agreed. I enquired:

- Are you safe right now?
- Where are you currently?
- Do you have access to your children?
- Do you know how to get to the closest police station?

After determining that she was in a safe spot with her children, we ended the call. I had promised her to find a safe house for her and her children. While waiting to hear back from my sources, I took a moment to reflect on the absurdity of this situation.

Without thinking, I knew exactly what questions to ask her and how to help her navigate a real-life horror story like this. Unfortunately, I knew what external threats felt like. I had an established and practiced protocol for it because of what had happened a decade earlier.

Back in 2011, Vesper's injury devastated me for months. I blamed myself for her accident and felt ashamed. Back then, I didn't feel like I was worthy of support or help, so I isolated myself. I surrendered to depression and moved into the dark forest for three months. I was so alone with my pain, drowning in my "mistakes" and undeservedness. My father's words echoed in my mind: "Who do you think you are, anyway? You're nobody, and you deserve nothing. You're nothing without my approval."

I was sitting alone in the darkness of my pain and shame, dying to hear that I was important and that I mattered. With that thirst for validation, I became an easy target for an abuser. Sadly,

I attracted a delusional, narcissistic stalker. Amid my dark forest, I saw a light in them that I misinterpreted as kindness.

I had made Vesper's injury all about myself. I felt like her injury was a confirmation that I was nothing and deserved nothing. I was drowning in depression and looking for any relief. There are reasons we can't trust our depressed selves for good decision-making: it draws us back to our old patterns of disempowerment.

The stalker, like any narcissist, took their time to love-bomb me. They drew me in by making me feel special and like I was worthy despite Vesper's injury. I felt alive and genuinely believed that this person would be in my life permanently. They **seemed** to help me let go and get over my pain. After years of anguish and hiding, I realized that a "helping hand" is not always there to help you. Sometimes, it's there to drown you.

This person I met in my dark forest was luring me to their campground by telling me they would never hurt or leave me. But what they meant was that I would never be allowed to hurt or leave **them**. I was about to enter a story that was no longer mine to write.

I brushed it off as no big deal the first time they turned on me because "they were just having a bad day." I justified the emotional abuse by telling myself that others had mistreated them and that they were just having a hard time. I made excuses for their behavior. The person I had known myself to be before Vesper's injury was slipping through my fingers.

After a while, their behavior became unacceptable. The bouts of "bad days" turned into weeks and then months. Out of some hidden vein of self-preservation, I found the strength to stand up for myself. I told this abusive person that if their offensive behavior did not change, I would cut them out of my life. They changed their behavior for a week, and then, for whatever reason, the emotional abuse started again. There was always an excuse behind every eruption. Perhaps you can relate to this, too.

When I confronted the abuser and held them accountable for their hurtful behavior, they started gaslighting me. Much like my aunt's reaction ten years later, the abuser told me I was just imagining things. Initially, I took their word at face value and thought I must have overreacted. Yet, after three or four gaslighting incidents, I saw their behavior for what it was: they were trying to unseat my sense of reality to get me under their spell and control.

"F**k this," I said to myself and told them that our shared connection was over. I thought I was safe because they lived on the other side of the world, but that wasn't the case. They traveled to Ireland and turned up at my clinic. They were harassing my clients to see when I would be coming out. They showed up at my places of leisure, attempting to dominate every space they entered. It was clear that they would not stop when they showed up at my residence and talked my landlords into letting them into my home.

I spent New Year's Eve of 2011 at the police station in Wicklow Town, Ireland, giving a five-hour statement about the threats and harassment. The Gardaí were courteous and kind, and they took me seriously. How could they not? I had laid out all the evidence of this person's behavior, including chains of one-sided psychotic messages and time stamps of their physical stalking.

The police told me they'd seen too many situations where the victim didn't reach out early enough. Sadly, they often ended up hospitalized or dead. The officers advised me to call the emergency number immediately if I thought anything was wrong in my environment. I promised to do so.

The next day, the stalker confronted me again. Feeling supported by my interaction with the police the night before, I felt I had some agency over how I would be treated. I took a deep breath, gave the stalker the senior constable's card, and told them that the Gardaí wished to speak with them. I also took my phone out and called 1-1-2. While the stalker stood beside me, I explained the situation to the operator, who told me the police were ten minutes away. The stalker overheard the conversation and fled.

Upon his arrival, the Senior Sergeant informed me they would press charges against the stalker for harassment. Further, the police would bring down the full force of the law on this person. They were looking at ten years in prison. The Gardaí's professional attitude abolished any doubt in my mind that I had been right to seek help. It reassured me that this was a serious issue and cemented my resolve to get this person out of my life, no matter what it took.

I learned my lesson. If we live in victim-consciousness and are vulnerable enough, we may invest years of our lives in relationships based on lies and abuse. That was certainly the case for me in Ireland after Vesper's injury. Ten years later, a similarly abusive and potentially dangerous reality was unfolding for my student in Sydney, Australia.

The Gardaí had been caring but realistic. They'd told me to keep safe at all times, keep my beloved close to me, and have an escape route available. Back then, they'd taught me the protocol I would pass on to my student. I was only hoping that it wasn't too late for her.

Instead of getting lost in the shadows of others, we must learn to see them in the transparency of daylight. It's easy to get swept away by someone who seems to love us. But let's be sober. Let's look at the person and their conduct before allowing them into our innermost circle. And if you discover an unsafe person in your inner circle, take a moment and devise an exit plan.

No matter how much it looks like we don't have power over real threats in the world, we do. If we learn to bet on ourselves and stay resilient and connected, we can defeat the darkness of those who wish us harm. To keep you safe, I recommend these two habits:

1. Grow safe spaces in your life wherever you can. If we live long enough, we will get tricked by those with an ulterior agenda. That's when our safety net comes into play.
2. Share your knowledge and experiences openly. While being betrayed by manipulative abusers can make us feel ashamed and isolated, talking about our experiences can empower us and others.

Chapter 32

SAFE SPACES

"We can't be brave in the big world
without at least one small safe space
to work through our fears and falls."

- BRENÉ BROWN

*P*AIN IS UNIVERSAL, AND PEOPLE who are feeling hurt will often end up injuring others. But healing is also universal, and when we heal, and when it's appropriate and welcomed, we can also help others heal.

Each of us who has been hurt has a choice to make. Will I do what my abusers did and take the easy way out by blaming others and simply passing on the hurt? Or will I do my work, stop the harm here, and support others who need it? The third option is to become a complicit bystander, knowing that I could have done something and should have. I had to make a conscious decision with my student whose life had been turned upside down.

For me, the choice was apparent but not easy. Of course, I was going to help my student and her family. But it wasn't lost on me that helping her was challenging and potentially even dangerous for me. What if I helped my student and her ex-husband came after me? Was I willing to risk my safety for this brave woman and her children?

My phone rang, and I found out I had secured a safe house for my student. I took a deep breath and dialed her number. First, I shared the safety protocol I had learned from the police in Ireland:

1. Keep an eye on your tail. If you think someone is following you, drive around a block and see if the car stays behind you the whole way around.
2. Call the emergency number and tell them you are being followed.
3. Tell them your location and ask them where the nearest police station is.
4. Then, ask them to inform the police that you are on your way there and that you and your children need protection.

Then, I asked her to repeat back to me what I said to ensure she'd got it. She did, thanked me, and told me she had a place lined up for a few days. I also told her about the place I had secured for her, and she promised to let me know if she needed it. Within days, she informed me that with the help of his parents, her ex had paid off his drug debt and that she and her children were no longer a target.

After that, the situation settled down. My student's ex-husband got help, and the legal system held him accountable for his activities. After she knew that her children were safe, my student went on to empower herself through her struggle. She chose to grow through the pain and is now empowering other victims of domestic violence to break free from their toxic situations. She brings real-life skills and hope for healing to those struggling behind closed doors. She is passing on her powerful learnings just like I did with mine. This incredible woman took what life had dealt her and made it into something significant. The legacy of her pain is now a beacon of light for others. Her work shows others that they, too, can come out of hiding.

This daisy chain of support is not an unusual occurrence. People who have healed from their trauma can feel a profound sense of gratitude for those who helped them. This gratitude often turns into an act of service as the recovered individual pays their gifts forward to someone else in need.

Like it does for most of us, helping someone on this fundamental level touched my soul and spirit in a way I had not expected. While the student's experience was heartbreaking, terrifying, and dangerous, and it was distressing to witness, helping her in this way felt significant. Over the next few days, I tuned into how I had helped this woman. Being able to offer her a safe space was not only practical. It felt consequential as well. As I sat with the sense of significance, I started to feel increasing levels of vocational vitality. Based on my past purpose-related pivots, this verve would illuminate a fast-approaching meaningful change in no time.

For the first time since finishing the production of the 4 People Within® course, I started to feel a firm resolution around a work project. Helping my client in this very practical yet emotionally significant way ignited a flame of passion in my heart. It felt "right" somehow to have the ability to offer safe spaces to people who needed them the most.

If you are highly intuitive, you know what I mean when I say my mind kicked into gear. I sat with my thoughts and feelings, and new ideas about safe spaces streamed into my consciousness quickly. Sometimes, I had to take a break from thinking because I could not keep up with what felt like a universal download directly from the source of life. I took breaks to meditate on the deeper meaning of my thoughts. When I humbled myself and asked the universe to show me what I needed to do next, an idea started to take shape in my soul.

The first ideas were around creating a series of "safe houses" worldwide. The vision felt too grand for me. I saw a McDonald's-like chain of safe havens and then realized the impracticality of it. If I wanted to offer people an opportunity to feel safe, heal, regroup, and change the tracks of their lives, I would not be able to advertise them openly.

Has this ever happened to you? You get an idea that feels right for you, but when you start developing it, you come up with many reasons why it won't work. Because I didn't see a clear way forward, I marginalized my "safe house" idea as a "silly, childlike idea of attempting to rescue everyone." My father's belittling messages unseated me for a moment, but within seconds, I could reparent myself out of the self-sabotaging thoughts. I reminded myself that my life belonged to me. I activated each of the four people within me, rolled up my sleeves, and got to work. I took a step back and looked at my life so far. These facts stood out as helpful for my vision:

Fact 1: I already knew what real estate investing was. I had owned several pieces of property in the past as a way of creating passive income. Thus, I could find the right places for the right prices. So, from that perspective, my idea was sound.

Fact 2: I was already working in the field of personal empowerment. I supported individuals to heal and become the best version of themselves. This would help them overcome difficult times and build a life that looked more like them.

Fact 3: I had the skills to promote safety in my life and the lives of others. I knew firsthand what hiding felt like. After the stalker issue in Ireland, I moved to Australia, and the same stalker found me there, too. After that, I put in place some severe safety protocols. My experience has taught me - on a deeply personal level - what it's like to live in hiding until you are strong and resourceful enough to step back into your life. I had already used the concept of a "safe house" in my own life by moving around and rarely disclosing my locations.

My grand vision of "safe houses" included Australasian, European, and North American properties. The houses would be in discrete locations. The doors were open to people who were genuinely ready to change. The residents could escape their old lives, come stay for six months to a year, re-establish themselves, learn to grow their own food, and maybe even study a new profession.

Yes, my vision was big. But I also knew that if I wanted to realize it, I had to stop marginalizing myself and trust my inner wisdom. I had felt the vitality of great ideas in the past, and they had turned out well. I had to decide to trust my wisdom while keeping it practical and realistic. At the very least, I could investigate the idea further and see if it would find wings.

Chapter 33

SAFE HOUSES

"Don't criticize somebody else
for what they're not doing.
You be it. Be about it. Be about
that action and go do it.
Keep your eye on your intention."

- BEYONCÉ KNOWLES-CARTER

THE IDEA WAS DEVELOPING, BUT I also had a practical challenge. Building a stalker-proof life had left me exhausted and financially drained. I was "should-ing" myself to build my idea from the ground up perfectly and immediately, and I didn't want to give myself time to recover.

Little by little, I broke down the old conditioning of self-sabotage and learned to reprioritize my health. In the many internal conversations I had about sacrificing myself at the altar of someone else, I repeatedly returned to the fact that facing a challenge did not mean that I had failed. For heaven's sake - I hadn't really started yet!

The problem was that my idea was not viable for attracting serious investors, at least not yet. If I wanted others to invest in my vision, I had to show them a more detailed plan and clearly communicate about the difference their investment would make in the lives of others. Right there and then, the details, plans, and numbers just weren't there.

For two months, I gathered more information and ideas. I wanted to see how much I could downscale my safe house vision without losing the essence of the project. I looked at properties in different countries, started creating operations manuals and projections for costs and donations, and concluded that there wasn't even a small-scale way of beginning to bring my vision to life. Not at this time. Maybe I could have raised the money; I simply wasn't ready. I had more recovery to do before I was able to fire on all cylinders, and before I could ask investors to commit to my vision! So, I accepted I had to bench the idea of global safe houses for now and focus on my current state of health and business affairs.

Like so often in life, when we keep our vision alive but surrender the "hows," we open ourselves up for new opportunities. When we stop focusing on how things *should be*, we start to flow with life, and our subconscious mind begins to paint a picture of how things *can be*.

The shift of focus helped me. By recommitting to my health and already existing business ideas, I could allow the Safe House vision to mature organically. Instead of "This is the only way I can build it," I started saying, "What don't I already know?" and "How else could the vision become a reality?". Instead of saying, "I'm not ready for investors," I started saying, "I am open to new ways in which this will come about."

Yes, I was sure of my vision, but I didn't want to control the process. I was committed to working hard but not forcing it. I wanted to enter the flow and allow life's magic to bring about the necessary resources. Luck truly is preparation meeting opportunity. I had some more preparation to do. If I wanted to see the future safe house residents heal, learn to love themselves, and share their inner genius with the world, I would have to do the same!

Thankfully, I also knew that a fixed mindset of "This is how it has to be" would bring me many more problems than solutions. By not forcing it, I could put my idea on the table and walk around it as I viewed and brainstormed the vision from different perspectives. This flexibility, I knew from many past experiences, would bring about a more thorough solution and multiple opportunities. I knew that perspectives like "Here's what could happen" and "Any number of other things can happen that I'm not yet aware of" allowed my intuition and intellect to create a new solution from "thin air."

But, of course, the ideas don't actually come from nothing. Great ideas come at the crossroads of hard work and clear intent. So, that's what I did. I worked hard on my health and current projects, and held my "safe house" vision without knowing how it would come about. I stayed open to the possibility of a great solution, and guess what happened? Yeah, you got it. One morning, while walking the dogs, I had a profound epiphany.

Walking on the track, I saw our then nineteen-year-old Sambotamus take off into the bushes. His age made him increasingly deaf, so I had to go find him. The only thing Sambotamus could hear clearly was the fridge door opening. This observation made me wonder if he had a condition called "selective hearing," where the dog only hears what he wants to hear.

The trickster Sambotamus is always up to something!

As I pulled our deceitful little dog out of the bushes, I saw a colony of ants. The movement around the mound reminded me of the old analog TV screen before the programming started for the day. Black and white "ants" were crawling manically across the screen, hypnotizing our senses to look for patterns within their movement. But what I had was a live, colored version of the show. For a moment, my mind went blank. It was almost like I performed a factory reset on the hard drive of my thoughts. For that moment of mesmerizing chaos, I let go of all the "cant's" and "shouldn'ts" of my mind. My thoughts went from ants to screens to computers in a matter of seconds, and I realized there **was** a way to have a "safe house" right here and right now: I could build a prototype online!

I thanked our little dog and got excited about the possibilities this idea presented:

1. I could roll up my sleeves and build a version of my vision immediately!
2. I had already come across an online community-building format that I liked and that was end-user-friendly. I could feel this idea's energy rise through and fuel me beyond excitement.
3. The online format could be my small-scale prototype to showcase my vision to potential investors. Any future transition from online to a brick-and-mortar "safe house" would be much less risky when the procedures were already in place.

Once again, trusting life and tuning into nature had shown me a way forward. I had stopped demanding that life work around me and relaxed into its natural flow. When I stopped resisting, life told me how to solve my problem elegantly and authentically. By trusting nature's divine order and timing, an implementable idea for my global string of safe spaces was born.

Every great vision brings about unlimited opportunities to succeed. Every great concept also brings about endless opportunities for us to either mature or continue to sabotage ourselves with our old patterns of pain. My newly found clarity brought up some old and new insecurities to my awareness. Was I recovered enough? I agonized over my physical ability to carry out the vision. I was worried about failing, and being ridiculed and rejected. On more than a dozen occasions, I wondered if I had what it took to turn my dream into a reality.

As I tuned into these questions, a quiet but confident inner voice told me that I could pace myself. I could build my vision one small step at a time, but if I wanted to succeed in this project, I had to overcome my insecurities, focus on the vision, and learn to let go of parts of my life that didn't support it. I would have to learn to manage my time better. I had to ensure that I was protecting my emotional environment from others' unhelpful input. Whether they were just interrupting my focus or directly undermining my vision, the result would be the same. I also had to line up a group of supportive people to ensure my physical and psycho-emotional well-being at this pivotal time of my life. As I was building something that needed my complete focus, joy, compassion, creativity, and effectiveness, I had to set well-thought-out and loving boundaries with everyone, including myself.

I knew these new boundaries on my energy would affect my relationships. I expected my die-hard inner circle to step in to support me, and those who wanted life to remain the same would not be happy. I anticipated that in every moment of "outing" my vision, I would sense my temptation to recoil and continue to play small just to keep the peace. But in my heart, I also knew that if I wanted to live authentically, loss would be inevitable.

I was about to find out who my real friends were.

Chapter 34

KNOW WHO YOUR FRIENDS ARE

"Isn't it strange, How people can change?
From strangers to friends,
Friends into lovers,
And strangers again."

- CELESTE | STEPHEN WRABEL
| JAMIE HARTMAN

You know that saying: speak the truth, even if your voice shakes? My hands shook when I surrendered to the energy of creation, committed to rolling up my sleeves and getting to work. While my body was taking the steps my heart dictated, my brain was reluctant to share my big vision with others.

Speaking to others about the safe houses was scary. I oscillated between being firm and on purpose, to not feeling like I had my own voice. I decided only to share my vision with my partner and my team because I knew I wasn't ready to come out with it fully. My partner backed me one hundred percent. My team was entirely on board and firmly behind me, or so I thought. I worked hard for months to build the platform, train the team, and create content. The energy source I had tapped into with the help of our little Sambo dog was fueling me to keep going.

Were there bad days? Of course. But my commitment to the vision was so strong that getting back on track was easy. Although we were making significant progress in building our online safe house, there was something that just didn't feel right. Although my then-business partner said all the right words, I felt increasingly alone with our vision. I felt like we were moving in different directions. My past partner's engagement in the dream was fragmented. They also seemed to follow through less and less with their duties. I started wondering if they had an agenda of their own.

Then, I started receiving emails from some of our students. They independently verified that my concerns about this partner were valid. I realized that the person I had trusted explicitly was using me instead of supporting me. They had started funneling team members and students from our organization to another one. They had roped another member of my immediate team into their plan. I knew this could happen. I just didn't think it would happen to me.

I've always been a devoted team player, so true to form, I tried to resolve the issues. I offered extra support and training to the individuals I knew were engaged in the game of deception. The more I gave, the less I received in return. It dawned on me that I was being taken advantage of by people who were supposed to protect our shared vision of a more joyous, compassionate, creative, and effective world for us and future generations. I was devastated.

I contacted my mentor, Kevin, a seasoned business consultant and a coach to many Fortune 50 companies. He pointed out that whether I was in an abusive business relationship or those team members lacked situational awareness, the end result was still the same: Disingenuous people drained my valuable resources, and my vision was compromised. It was also possible that I was failing to protect our students from their corrosive influence and lying.

Kevin recommended that I take a direct stance with them and ask them straight up, "What is going on?".

This was precisely what I needed to hear. It became clear that devotion had been a one-way street with these people. I was sad to realize that I had willingly entered into a relationship with these people, and had allowed their destructive conduct due to my brain injury, naïveté, and blind faith. If you've ever been in one-sided relationships, you know how shocking the realization is and how hard it can be to break that pattern. The longer you have allowed toxic behavior to go on, the more difficult setting boundaries becomes.

First, there's disbelief. When you start standing up for yourself, some may fail to take you seriously. Then, if the other person is not willing to hear you, they are not willing to resolve the issue. This leaves **you** to solve the problems, even those you didn't directly create. At this stage, the other person usually takes either a victim's or a persecutor's stance. Either way, you'll often end up having to clean up their emotional reaction before even attempting to resolve the issue itself.

Demanding respect from others is not as simple as telling them what you want. It also means that you must respect yourself, and enforce the boundaries as many times as it takes. When you insist on being treated with dignity, you will have to renegotiate most of your existing boundaries. Renegotiating boundaries requires two people in good faith to come together and listen to one another. To succeed, both people must take the feedback seriously rather than personally. Both parties must also want to resolve the issue proactively. If only one person is mature or proactive in their approach, the relationship becomes yet another unbalanced power dynamic.

Armed with Kevin's wisdom, I was ready to confront the issue. I centered myself before speaking with the two team members I suspected of foul play. I brought along emails from multiple students and our mission statement to exhibit to them that there was nowhere to go but to the heart of the matter. The whispers around unprofessional conduct, back-handed business dealings, and poaching students had turned from scattered fragments of information into verifiable facts.

When I spoke with the whistleblower students, I believed them and was forced to admit a pattern. These students were not connected to one another, but their reports were almost identical. Our students' passion for a more joyous, compassionate, creative, and effective world was being used to advance these fallen team members' personal agendas. I thanked the students for coming forward and made sure to do what I could to repair any trust that may have been broken between us. I was thankful that our students' faith in me was so strong that they felt comfortable reporting any off-brand behavior to me directly. They knew that I would want to know and that I would fix it.

When I asked the two team members to explain the reports from our students, they denied that anything dodgy was going on. They denied having the conversations with our students that had been reported back to me. This, to me, smelled like gaslighting.

Thankfully, I knew this pattern well: deny, delay, and normalize. The experiences with my family and the stalker taught me to check my facts before entering into any discussions. This would block the other person's deny and delay. It would also keep everyone on track with the points so that alternative facts could not be normalized.

Back when I worked with lawyers to get a restraining order against the stalker, I learned something invaluable. When you think someone is lying, only ask questions you know the answers to and can prove. Don't rely on your perception of what is going on. Don't believe your opinion about the situation. After all, an opinion is the lowest form of knowledge. Instead, get the facts and proof before you ask questions or make accusations.

I wanted to give these two a final chance to repair the rupture their conduct had caused in our relationships and on our team.

But instead of an open and honest dialogue, they became defensive and shut down. It became apparent very quickly that there was no turning back. The two knew I had caught them and were unwilling to discuss changing their ways.

Based on their response to raising these issues, I decided I would not continue to prompt them to do the right thing. Our time together was over. These people were not interested in working proactively to repair any injury their lying and shoddy business practices had caused. I let these two key team members go and went on to manage the chaos they left behind.

Has this ever happened to you? Have you discovered something unexpected about someone you thought you knew and could trust? Have you had to clean up after someone else and their mess? It can be such a disorienting experience. If this is you, I see you. You deserve nothing less than honesty, openness, and clear communication. But if transparency is not on offer freely, you may have to create it for yourself by clarifying your priorities and setting boundaries by exercising your inner power.

Chapter 35

PRIORITIZE AND EXECUTE

"Prioritize your problems and take
care of them one at a time, the highest
priority first. Don't try to do everything
at once, or you won't be successful."

- JOCKO WILLINK

HEART-BREAKINGLY, AT THE SAME TIME, we also had to say
goodbye to three of our rescue horses. Our Sisu horse's chronic
hoof took an unexpected turn for the worse, and the other two,
Trigger and Missy, had been on end-of-life treatment since the
previous winter.

With that, I felt like two of my life's three most important parts
were falling apart. My business nearly folded, and my beloved
equine friends were gone. The only thing that stood strong was
my personal relationships. Honestly, I don't know what I would
have done had I lost my partner or one of my key confidants at
that time.

If you have ever run a team that breaks apart, you understand
how fractured the remaining relationships can become. The people
who leave will likely badmouth the business and manipulate the
staff who stay. And those devoted people who stayed may struggle

with trusting the company's future. They may also have a hard time setting healthy boundaries with their ex-teammates.

The dynamic left behind was highly toxic and destructive. If you have gone through anything similar, you can understand why I nearly gave up on my vision for the online safe house. The whirlwind of gut punches was just too much. It's not easy to be both creative and feel betrayed and grief-stricken. I was incredibly fortunate that three of my five key team mates stayed on. I would not have had the strength to carry on without this dynamic trio.

Looking back, I had put too much faith in the wrong people around me, and in hindsight, I wish I had set better boundaries with them from the very beginning. Needless to say, I have also become more realistic about giving people multiple chances. My mentors no longer need to criticize me for exercising too much patience.

As my business partner was gone, it was up to me to decide how to dig ourselves out of this hole. I had to think clearly if I wanted my vision to survive these losses. In practical terms, it meant that:

1. I had to separate and prioritize my grief. I had to differentiate between the grief of losing my horses and the pain of my misplaced trust. There was no way I could make sense of both losses simultaneously. I had to pick which pain was more significant and deal with that first. Then, after having worked through the first grief, I could find some balance and work on letting go of the second loss. I appreciate that others would have done this differently, but I prioritized the grief for my beloved horses first. In hindsight, I'm glad I did. It was the right decision for me.
2. I had to stop making excuses for others' bad behavior. I had given these incredible, broken horses a loving forever home, and they deserved it. But you know what? People who lie and deceit do not deserve my kindness and

devotion. I do not hold a crutch, but I also don't nurture relationships that show no earnest effort of honesty and reciprocation.

3. Not all relationships are created equal; some will be more meaningful and tender than others. Some will be brief encounters to spark an insight within us. But all relationships reflect who we are in this moment or what lessons we must learn at this time. Intuitively, I knew that if I wanted my vision of the "safe houses" to succeed, I had to cut the abusive and one-sided relationships out of my life.

4. I had to fully commit to my vision instead of making a pledge to the people who came and went. It was a harsh lesson to learn, but making this commitment to the mission has helped me keep my focus on the vision.

Like many survivors of childhood abuse, my conditioning told me that setting boundaries was selfish and hurtful. But that's not true! My life - and the lives of those I love - changed for the better when I started prioritizing myself and setting boundaries with myself and others. By prioritizing and executing my well-thought-out boundaries, I created a culture around me that is nurturing for everyone, not just for everyone except me.

Self-care is not selfish! Self-care makes sure that everyone wins, including you! If you struggle to prioritize your needs, remember that self-care becomes possible when you understand that we are all connected, and that to look after others is to look after yourself first. This is true physically, psychologically, emotionally, and, yes, financially too.

As Bono says, "We are one, but we're not the same." In other words, if I wanted success for others, I had to give it to myself, too. I had to model something I was encouraging others to do and not simply do the hard work on their behalf. If I didn't look after my own well-being day-to-day, my interactions with others would always be one-sided.

Know your priorities, and be willing to take action to fulfill them. Habitual self-sacrifice does not lead to success. In my case, it led to being used for others' agendas. Imagine how bad the situation could have been. Our students, too, would have been used as pawns in others' games. Yes, I have the right to protect myself. But most of all, like anyone who has been trusted to lead others, I have the **duty** to protect them.

Sacrificing ourselves at the altar of others does not only hurt the people you want to protect. It depletes our most fundamental source of creative energy and the most significant asset we will ever own: ourselves.

Part V

HOME

Chapter 36

ACKNOWLEDGE YOUR POWER

"The power is within you."

- LOUISE HAY

MANY BELIEVE THAT POWER **ONLY** comes from privilege and big job titles. I can't entirely agree. While privilege - race, gender, orientation, skin color, and education - certainly gives some of us an inside track, there is a more significant determining factor at play. Becoming powerful is determined by our capacity to acknowledge our inner strength and our decision to utilize it. It is not lost on me that I am a white woman making this statement. I apologize if my words hurt you. They are not my opinion but a direct reflection of tens of thousands of conversations with people from **all** walks of life.

I also discovered from these conversations that you can immediately start wielding your mighty sword of creation by making more intentional decisions about your everyday life. I have come to believe that small but well-thought-out daily decisions and actions are the most accurate determinant of our success in life.

Sure, taking the time to make big life decisions is essential. But if we only focus on the "big deals" in our lives and disengage from the small details, we can easily overlook the tortoise and the hare concept. The small everyday decisions - and actions - build a solid foundation for our personal power and success.

Consistent, small, and positive decisions form our self-affirming and nurturing habits over time. For example, making a good decision about your breakfast fuels the rest of your day. Consistent good choices about your breakfast contribute to creating a healthy body and a happier life.

Some still think that the amount of water you drink doesn't matter. But you probably know that it determines how well your body eliminates toxins that cloud your judgment. That's why a consistent and thoughtful hydration habit helps your brain stay healthy and your thoughts flexible. This small, often overlooked habit may even lessen your anxiety and stress over time.

Taking a brisk fifteen-minute walk before you start that critical work project can make all the difference in the clarity of communication. Similarly, allowing yourself to nap instead of reaching for that extra cup of coffee gives your brain a much-needed opportunity to clean itself. Taking every occasion to make good micro-decisions nurtures your natural inner genius and allows it to emerge.

You might think, "Oh no, I've been letting myself go for way too long, and there's simply too much to change! I can't possibly change everything about my life straight away! It's way too much." I hear you! Coming to terms with your past passivity can be confronting. Realizing that everyday micro-decisions have the power to build a successful life can initially be overwhelming.

Striving for absolute perfection from the get-go is a recipe for disaster. While we may be able to reach moments of excellence in our lives, perfection is not something we are meant to maintain indefinitely. Even if we could, it would soon lose its appeal, and we would reach for another level of perfection and accomplishment. Doing your best now is the perfect outcome for now and will always be enough. Humans are growth-seeking beings that never stop evolving, and failing is an essential part of that evolution.

Considering that you make more than thirty-four thousand decisions daily, it would be improbable that you - even if you wanted to - could make each of them perfect. Additionally, as we grow, our desires change. Thus, achieving perfection is an illusion because once we accomplish our goals, our inner vision for bigger and better things in life gets activated.

Understanding this may help you see the futility of striving for perfection. Even if you succeeded, in no time, you would want something else, and then your picture would be imperfect again. I'm not saying that we should not strive for excellence. By all means, choose the level of performance that is right for you at this time, but don't judge yourself for not being perfect.

So, let's elevate our health, wealth, relationships, and vocation by choosing a few micro-habits to focus on. Change takes time because establishing new, positive habits takes time. Your brain needs thoughtful repetition to rewire itself for success. After a while, these intentionally built new neural pathways keep our good practices going automatically. The amount of deliberate repetition determines how quickly and firmly the new success habit sticks. Focusing on carrying out the practice for ninety days without judging yourself for "not being there yet" will keep you on track.

Have you ever made a New Year's resolution only to give up on it by mid-February? We give up on our well-thought-out decisions and goals too early because we don't allow our brains to rewire themselves through practice. Thankfully, accountability with a friend or a mentor can keep us on track, especially when things get tricky!

After about ninety days, the positive, thoughtful habit becomes automatic, the reel of our lives changes for the better, and we begin to see a difference. As a result, our confidence and sense of achievement increase, and we begin to make new, even more beneficial choices about our habits.

The decision to change is just the first step. Being able to keep going shouldn't have to be up to your willpower alone. Success breeds success. Reflecting back on your past achievements in life can give you a leg-up when you are failing forward, or facing stressful times. But intentionally building positive habits is like putting money in the bank. It can keep you afloat while traveling through life's choppy seas.

What power-inducing habit you tap into first is up to you! I categorize my habits into four groups:

- physical,
- psychological,
- emotional, and
- spiritual.

My well-functioning physical vessel is maintained by ensuring that I get enough water, movement, sleep, and food and that my circulation, digestion, and elimination processes work correctly.

The basics of optimal psychological health mean understanding and making most of my cognitive preferences, having the freedom of thought and expression, and practicing critical thinking when making life decisions, big and small.

For an easy-to-navigate emotional landscape, I need healthy habits of self-discovery and acceptance, authentic connection with myself and others, a healthy sense of belonging, and loving boundaries.

To live a healthy spiritual experience, I need the habits of presence, connection, openness, and creativity.

Now, you go! What are your needs in these four categories? Do you have other categories you have added to your list? Whatever way you decide to start claiming your power is perfect for you. You are a sovereign being, and you have the right to choose the right habits and decisions for you. You are important.

So, acknowledge your power by claiming a habit and creating a practice around it. Remember to learn as you go! You can only fail at claiming your power by giving it up.

Chapter 37

THE LIGHT WITHIN YOU

"It's the moment you think
you can't, that you can."

- CÉLINE DION

CHANGING YOUR HABITS IS NOT always easy. There are a million reasons why we withhold doing what we know is good or right for us. In fact, you may say, "That's all good and dandy, Merja, but what if I'm not in that happy-clappy space where I can just start changing my habits? What if I'm in a space of despair or depression? What if I still don't believe I *can* do this?"

Matey, I hear you. It's been more than once or twice that I have felt that, too! I, too, have felt the freeze of disempowerment and the overwhelm of not knowing where to start. I felt like I had to discover the "why" of my struggle before I was able to do something about it. If this is you, I understand. I'm one of those people who needs to understand before taking action. If you are struggling with not knowing what is holding you back, using my own experiences, I developed a tool that may help you. I call it Inner Parenting, reparenting, or the 4 People Within®.

In short, the 4 People Within® encourages you to discover the grown-up and the Inner Child parts of you. Most often, this confusion of "who is talking" overwhelms us and freezes us into inaction. Understanding each of these people and how they operate has the power to stop the overwhelm and start the healing process.

Each of the 4 People Within®'s voices is distinctly different from one another, and when you recognize who is speaking, you can identify and fulfill their needs. Leading-edge psychologists assign most of our depression, anxiety, post-traumatic stress, and trauma to unfulfilled needs and expectations we carry. When our basic needs for safety, shelter, food, sovereignty, belonging, and self-actualization are not met, we cannot be ourselves fully.

In Chapter 1, I wrote that your greatest gifts to the world lie beneath your deepest wounds. As long as I felt the weight of my trauma, this sentence made no sense to me. If you, like me, have experienced severe abuse, you may not see how this statement could possibly be true. If that's your experience right now, I get it. I hear you.

But, like me, with proper support and tools, you can reclaim the power and acknowledge the light that shines within you. Through this work, I realized that when we learn to meet our own needs, we can offer ourselves the support and safe spaces we need to learn, heal, and grow into our whole selves. Through the 4 People Within® Inner Parenting work, I learned how to love and support myself in a way I never experienced as a child. It wasn't until I reparented myself that I began to see the gifts that lie beneath my deepest wounds. The past generations did the best they could with the knowledge, experience, and support they had. However, that still left me injured.

Once I reparented myself, I could recognize and nurture the genius within me. You, too, have this genius within you, no matter how broken you feel right now. You may not believe it, but I see it every day. Maybe you have seen it too: the most giving, kind, quiet people have the most profound treasures to share but - because of past trauma - aren't confident to show others what they are capable of. Discovering your inner light and learning how to let it shine can take a while, especially if you have experienced deep pain in your formative years.

Additionally, it's good to note that humans are contradictions in terms. While we are growth-oriented, we are also comfort-driven beings. We are literally hardwired to avoid getting hurt. Keeping others at arm's length can give us a sense of safety. We continue to protect ourselves fiercely until we realize that most people don't want to hurt us. If you're like me and have experienced abuse at a tender time in your life, the trauma can distort your beliefs about your capabilities or others' agendas. As survivors of abuse, we may not trust ourselves or misinterpret others' intentions to be worse than they are. This is yet another reason why breaking old patterns and creating new success habits can be difficult: the process is inherently complicated and dichotomous.

Breaking the cycle of victimhood is hard because once we are violated, the mark of the assault stays with us. It's a unique mark that only three types of people recognize: victims of abuse, highly empathic people, and predators. Knowing who to trust is complicated because both empaths and predators show up in very similar ways. I differentiate between the two by putting aside what people say and looking at what they do. Their actions eventually shed light on their motives, whether noble or abusive.

When we - over time - discover some safe people and spaces, we can begin our reparenting process, relax our defensive stance, and soften into the flow of life. Through Inner Parenting, I was able to let go of my victim story. This new, internal parental presence gave me confidence in myself, and I could stop super-imposing my past trauma onto others' behavior. The more I trusted myself and others, the more trustworthy people I encountered.

You see, our subconscious mind finds "evidence" of whatever we believe. Before reparenting myself, a person, situation, and conversation feels one way. But when you put down your armor of defensiveness, you begin to see yourself and others more clearly.

But getting to this point takes time, work, and support from those who have walked the healing path before you.

I decided to reparent myself, because I wanted more from life. Having left Finland and established myself in Ireland, I realized that the weight of my armor was too heavy to carry. I recognized that if I wanted to have a life of joy, compassion, creativity, and effective service, I had to learn ways to let go of my suspicion of others. Even after all the hurt and grief I had endured, I realized it was time to unwind that barbed wire around my heart and let myself live fully. I wanted all parts of me to be nurtured, not just "the good girl" who would always fix everything for everyone else. I wanted to learn how to relate to others lovingly and how to set caring, but healthy boundaries. I wanted to be seen as the person I was, not just the chameleon others were used to seeing.

I also wanted a calm and predictable home environment. I was tired of darting around the house, looking for evidence of how I had failed. I had exhausted myself by being hyper-vigilant. I wanted to be more intentional about my vision and goals instead of living only for others.

I wanted to have time to geek out on my interests guilt-free or have a cup of coffee without thinking I should do something "more productive" with my time. I wanted to feel more joy in life, and I wanted all parts of me to feel safe and loved.

My Inner Parent and I carefully chose my success habits and persevered with them even when going got tough. By setting four success habits per year around things I wished my parents had taught me, I matured into a more balanced and happy individual within just a few years. This approach was the best decision I made in my life. It helped me heal my childhood wounds, become a happy and functioning adult, and build a life that looked like me.

After establishing a good Inner Parenting foundation, I started using the method with my more significant life decisions. After the dishonesty and deception, I used my reparenting protocol to rebuild my team. By combining this tool with thoughtful choices and success habits, I began to see a growing amount of business success, deeply fulfilling professional relationships, and effective and ever-improving physical and mental health.

As I reparented myself, I let go of the past generations' pain, which wasn't mine to carry anyway. The 4 People Within® work also showed me how to put down others' expectations and be true to myself. Creating the self-parenting framework taught me how to create mutually caring, reciprocal relationships without self-sacrifice and power games. It was as if, for the first time in my life, the light within me recognized and wanted to honor the light within others.

The light within you needs air, fuel, and a point of ignition to keep burning. Getting to know your Inner Family helps you find everything you need to nurture your inner radiance. After you learn the basics, the four people within you can continue to evolve, and keep your inspired vision alive though tough times. So, start reparenting yourself by gently choosing success habits you can handle, and if you need help with your process, join us at Sumiloff.com! How would it feel if, instead of fretting about the future or thinking about the past, you could simply focus on living your dream life?

Chapter 38

WOULDN'T IT BE NICE IF...

"Life is supposed to feel good for you."

- ABRAHAM HICKS

*T*HE LAST CHAPTER MAY HAVE got your cogs turning. You may wonder, "What do I want from life?". When I'm in that space, I go back to basics and play a game I learned years ago from Abraham Hicks called "Wouldn't it be nice if...". Perhaps you would like to join me?

- **Wouldn't it be nice if... my relationships were mutually caring and inspired and allowed everyone to show up as their authentic selves?** How would your relationships change if everyone felt secure and loved, just as they were? Would there be fewer power games and hurtful interactions? Could you come together to create something meaningful instead of being defensive, feeling lonely, and ending up isolated?

The keys to honest, authentic, and reciprocal relationships are loving boundaries and kind but genuine communication. Understanding yourself and your needs, and learning how to communicate them effectively can resolve any relationship issue as long as every person involved is open to it.

It's said that it takes two to create a negative dynamic and only one to break it. I know how hard it can be to be the one breaking the pattern. I return to the 4 People Within® Inner Parenting approach whenever I struggle. For more times than I can count, tuning into - and providing for - my Inner Children's needs has given me the strength to continue transforming my relationships. Tuning into and encouraging my Inner Children to speak their truth lovingly has turned me from a people-pleaser to a conscious contributor to mutually respectful and authentic connections.

- **Wouldn't it be nice if... I could make effortless decisions that consistently built a better life for me and my loved ones?** How much easier would your everyday decisions be if you could activate healthy decision-making at will? Do you recognize times when others knowingly pull on your heartstrings because they know you'll make them feel better? Are your own goals and vision suffering because you are experiencing fear, nervousness, or feeling like you're not good enough?

The key is accurate and effective decision-making. Before being deliberate in choosing my success habits, my life was a messy landscape where I based all my decisions on how others felt about me. Now, with the guidance of critical thinking, I make communicative, strategic choices that propel my life - and the lives of those I care about - forward.

Critical thinking keeps your destructive feelings in check, while emotions aligned with the goal enrich your logical decision-making. When the two decision-making styles - thinking and feeling - work side by side, they maximize your capacity to be one with yourself and be of service to others - with good boundaries, of course!

I highly recommend implementing critical thinking in all decisions, big and small. Learning to embrace my inner thinker and teaching her necessary thinking skills helped me implement the most meaningful changes in my life. Asking questions, communicating your thoughts to trusted others, reflecting on the feedback, and adapting your approach can help you, too, make right decisions. Then, make sure that your plan is practical as well!

- **Wouldn't it be nice if... I had time and space to delve into my authentic interests with total commitment and without feeling like they were competing with the life I have already built?** Before your current responsibilities, what activities did you love losing yourself in? What plans would you make with yourself when nothing and no-one is putting pressure on you? How could you make your life more purposeful if you could take a moment to explore what is possible rather than just fight the fires of everyday life?

There are no shortcuts to achieving more space in your life. You simply have to claim it. You must decide that you are worthy of taking the time, even if it's only ten minutes every day. Your life is *your* life. Don't live it for others only. When you claim this time to explore personal interests, you will show up as a better, more focused version of yourself. Claim the time and book it into your diary.

This was a significant turning point in my Inner Parenting journey. As a result of reclaiming my time, I could both write and record the 4 People Within® course and parent myself through my PTSD triggering. Now, when I forget about myself and get busy with life and others' expectations of me, I return to the statement: "I have the right to claim my time. It's my life first and foremost".

- **And wouldn't it be nice if... I could experience joy daily while striving for my goals?** How would your life change if you committed to one intentional success habit every ninety days? Would you experience more safety, predictability, and security in your life? Would you learn what you wished you had been taught as a child? What four habits will bring you closer to your dream life this year? Is it health, wealth, relationships, or other life habits?

What success habits would make you feel joyous and creative while carrying them out? Would you enjoy swimming, running, or writing your own memoir? Can you study a subject of interest? Is there an opportunity to change your job to a more pleasurable one?

What success habits bring you closer to your life's goals? Other than happiness, what do you want to achieve in life? What is important to you, and what small habitual change can you create around it for the next ninety days?

Success breeds success. Observing ourselves making good decisions increases our level of confidence. If you have been down in the dumps for some time, you may find it hard to make good decisions or find the positives in your life. If that's the case, start small. For example, you can use this book as a tool to get going. I hope there has been something positive or supportive in it for you. Have you taken a pen or a highlighter and marked a page, a paragraph, a sentence, or even just a word that spoke to or encouraged you? Focus on the meaning it has given you, and if you can, decide to bring more of its essence into your everyday life from now on.

I know how hard it can be to imagine a life that is good for you, especially if you have experienced a lot of turmoil or heartbreak. But don't give up! It took me (what felt like) forever to climb out of the depression and anxiety I felt from being attacked and terrorized by the stalker. The gaslighting from my aunt simply made everything worse. I know how hard it can be to overcome familial friction, especially when those (older generations) who are supposed to protect you first neglect and then attack you instead. If this is you, please know you are not alone.

As you now know and have heard me say many times, change can be tricky. Make sure to stay intentional as you make one meaningful micro-decision after another. Some find journaling helpful. They keep a diary of every successful micro-decision so that they can see how far they have already come. If you are currently struggling, start small. I began by ensuring I drank at least two liters of water daily. That's it: no massive vision, no berating myself for my small goal. Instead, I encouraged myself by thinking, "Wouldn't it be nice if I got into the habit of drinking two liters of water daily?". This small step into the right direction was pressuring me to grow in self-awareness and care, but it was also easy enough to complete. Essentially, instead of biting off more than I could chew, I had set myself up to succeed comfortably.

There were days when the only thing I could do was to drink two liters of water. I marked those days a success. As I observed my success with that one small habit, it propelled me into completing another task daily, then another, and then another. Within a year, I had established a routine of hydrating, a practice of gentle movement, a process of self-establishment through Inner Parenting, and a pattern of good sleep hygiene. Effectively, my life had changed completely. I was thinking clearly, getting strong and flexible in my body, supporting myself emotionally and with good decision-making, and I got great rest. This can be you, too.

It bears repeating that success breeds success, and that positive momentum builds on itself. Small habits have a significant impact over time. Don't fool yourself into thinking that "perfect" or "fast" is better. It's not. The best way to guarantee success is to start small and be prepared to fail forward. Stay on track and stay stubborn. You got this!

Chapter 39

WHERE IS THE PONY?

"The B.S. that happens to you is
the fertilizer for your growth."

- MERJA SUMILOFF

*H*AVE YOU EVER BEEN CALLED stubborn, as if it's a bad thing to be tenacious? As we grow up, our teachers, parents, and other people in perceived positions of power want to make us easy to handle. Were you the kid in school who questioned everything only to be told to sit down and be quiet? Or were you the child that should "be seen and not heard," according to the old adage? Were you ever criticized for being headstrong and dogged?

One person's stubbornness is another person's steadfastness. A man in a boardroom who sticks to his guns is "tough," whereas a woman in the same position is "a b***h." If we buy into this dogma, we give up on the most critical form of stubbornness: determination.

What we tolerate, we normalize. Sometimes, we lack determination when dealing with the world or others in it. If we abandon our needs and simply allow others to determine who we are, we end up giving up on our self-advocacy and, thus, our purposeful life.

After a while of minimizing our own sovereignty, we begin to believe that we "aren't important" or "can't do _____ (fill in the blank)." I've certainly been there! Many, many times. These thoughts are a slippery slope to self-abandonment. Our lack of determination stops us from living the existence that feels nourishing for our souls.

When I talk about stubbornness, I don't mean being difficult or "too complicated" or any other derogatory statements others use for Pathfinders like us. I'm talking about steadfast and willful self-advocacy, knowing what I am and am not willing to tolerate, and for how long. If you are the same, never stop determining what is and isn't right for you!

On a macro level, women may give up their jobs because they feel pressured to have a family. An intuitive feeler may work in a loud environment simply because they need to put food on the table. Certainly, I have known a lot of equestrians who have caved in to "the normal way of doing things," even though they knew it was *not* the right way to train their horse.

When we zoom into our everyday lives, we can find micro versions of this toxic surrender everywhere. You may put up with a colleague's racist microaggressions at work because you don't like confrontation. You may put aside your need for reflection because more extroverted people want to move on with the tasks, and you don't speak up. You may skip time with your horses because those around you think it's just a hobby when, in fact, for you, it's a lifestyle.

We all react differently to these situations. You may freeze when someone crosses your boundary and keep pretending like nothing happened. Or you may get angry and go on the offense. Or you could look for ways to escape the uncomfortable situation, or start fawning at the person causing you pain. These are all prevalent and understandable responses to uncomfortable and scary situations.

In case you don't know, I want to point out that everyone has fears and insecurities. Every single person encounters difficulties and B.S. situations. The good news is that dealing with these situations is a skill. One that everyone can learn. That is if they want to.

You may wonder: is it better to make big life decisions like changing a job or leaving a relationship, or fix smaller problems such as standing up to daily microaggressions? It really depends on what your needs are, and what you are prepared to live with. The thought of big changes may feel liberating, but may also have undesired consequences. On the other hand, the micro changes, such as setting a boundary with a colleague, friend, or partner, may feel like it won't make any difference because you already know that they won't change - and you may be right! Life is complex, and relationships are messy. If you have loved and lost, you know what I mean.

Some relationships will grow with loving boundaries, and others may succeed by dying so both of you can move on. Only you know what is right for you, and what price you are willing to pay for your decisions. For example, I have ended relationships with friends because they wanted me to play a predetermined role. For me, it's not so important that we agree on everything but that we have the freedom to have our own perspectives. So, by all means, let's disagree, but where I draw a line is when others tell me what I should think or feel. I, like you, am a real person with my own perspective on everything.

And because I'm a real person, I have also been in situations where others have proved me wrong. There were times when I thought I had all the facts and that I was right. In fact, I was sure that I was right. This certainty now works as a red flag for me: the more confident I feel about being right, the more I have to study the opposing perspective. For example, when I believe I am the most intelligent person in the room, I will automatically begin to look for someone who knows more than I do.

I have learned to use this concept in reverse, too. Whenever I feel hopeless and like a failure, I question it. The more confident I feel I have nothing to offer, the more I look for evidence of the value I have already created in the world.

Similarly, when I feel like there is no way out of a sticky situation, I ask myself: "What don't I already know?" Feeling cornered doesn't mean there's no window behind the curtain on the wall. Whenever I feel cornered, I imagine the window, open it, and lower myself to the ground. Yes, I may feel dazed by the brightness of the day, and I don't know what's happening in the distance, but what I do know is that I am no longer cornered.

What about you? Have you ever thought you were the most intelligent or important person in the room, only to discover that you were wrong? Have you ever felt down in the dumps and someone tells you how awesome they think you are? Have you ever found the most curious way out of a dead-end situation? More often than not, persevering through life's challenges brings us to the other side of them: it brings us to wisdom.

But be aware! It's easy to get stubborn about the wrong things. Our toxic egos want us to be right instead of being happy. When I realized this, I decided to turn my stubbornness into a superpower. Instead of buying into my toxic ego's story, I use it to heal and grow. Being stubborn about self-advocacy and growth is a tool many rarely speak about, but one that may make or break it for you. If you're not your own best friend, then who is? Self-advocacy is not about being full of yourself. It's about being open to learning about yourself and recognizing the possibilities life offers for your healing, growth, and self-mastery.

For me, the most comforting self-advocacy process is my belief that every bad situation has something of value to teach me. I have seen this to be the case more times than I can list. I'm so convinced of this universal truth that any time life throws a wrench into my works, I simply state my surprise and start looking for the opportunity.

If you've been around me, you may have heard me tell this story: Once upon a time, there was a pair of sisters, twins. They were nine. One Christmas, their parents decided to teach the girls a valuable lesson. Instead of multiple presents of toys, books, and clothes wrapped beautifully, they gave each of them a pile of manure. One child looked at the parents with disgust, telling them that when she grew up, she would discuss this experience with her therapist. The other daughter started digging at her pile of poo. Her sister looked at her, exclaiming, "WHAT ARE YOU DOING!?". The girl looked up from her pile of manure, smiling, and said, "There's so much poop here. There has to be a pony in here somewhere!" She kept digging.

I found the pony!

Throughout my life, I have learned that unexpected challenges are not just B.S. If I'm flexible with what life throws my way, I can use the ingredients to my advantage. My own life experience has shown me that every proverbial pile of manure has a pony hidden in it. But I will only find it if I'm willing to heal what needs healing and then delve into the hidden learning. There is no space for my toxic ego in this process. And you know what else is great about manure? It's nature's fertilizer for growth! Now that I believe I'm worth nurturing, I want to take every opportunity to grow myself. Bring it on!

Like every stream creates a river, every time we can push our toxic ego aside, we create a better reality where we don't constantly give up on ourselves. Every good decision, positive reframing, and loving boundary we learn to set creates a reality where people respect and cherish us more. When life serves us what seems like a pile of manure, will you reject it, or will you start digging for the pony?

Committing to relentlessly pursuing yourself as a valuable asset means that you advocate for yourself without stomping on others' lives. You, the incredible, imperfectly perfect you, are the priceless treasure hidden in the manure of what happened to you, ready to be found. Is it time to start digging?

Chapter 40

WHO ARE YOU BECOMING?

"When we break loose from
our perceived limitations,
we have the freedom to discover
how much we can be."

- LINDA PARELLI

IF NOTHING WAS HOLDING YOU back, who would you be? Becoming who you are is as much about letting go of who you no longer want to be, as it is about knowing who you are underneath all the trauma and others' expectations.

In fact, letting go of the parts of us that no longer serve us is liberating. One of my most influential mentors, Linda Parelli, helped me with this concept. She challenged me to imagine my perfect day. She encouraged me to claim what was important to me and stop apologizing for it. I suspect she knew what I soon discovered: that as my success habits grow and solidify, one "perfect day" leads to another, and then another. Soon, I had a meaningful and focused month, a quarter, and a year. "Geez… is that how a happy life is created?" I wondered. Although it wasn't easy every day, the concept felt doable because it was so simple!

At first, I struggled to identify a perfect day. Then, when I allowed myself to imagine what it would look like, it was time to start setting boundaries around it. Essentially, I had to remove or delegate everything that wasn't it! When I began to ask for my day to be respected, I felt uncomfortable. Initially, I wasn't fluent in claiming my life without considering others' needs. But as I dove deeper into the challenge Linda had given me, the practice become more comfortable.

I realized that I had done this exercise before but had been using an avatar. Back in the day, when I was aiming to represent my country in the Olympics, my avatar was an Olympic winner and a full-time athlete. I used to make my daily decisions in line with what an Olympian would do. I prioritized my activities according to my vision. For example, would I, as a world-class event rider, go partying before a big competition? Unsurprisingly, the answer for me was "no."

Linda's exercise of a perfect day really spoke to me. It has been a profound tool to discovering my personal values and urging me to live by them in real life. My discovery of values was no longer theoretical. It became practical as well. If you're like me and you see the value in the exercise but struggle to claim your time and power, feel free to borrow my avatar approach!

So, look at your current situation. Who would be your avatar, and what kind of a day would they have? How would they deal with your current challenges, and what focus would they have? What would they change about your present life, and in what order? Even if you don't yet feel completely deserving, these questions can help you start planning your perfect day and begin to clarify the order of your upcoming success habits.

Next, be mindful of your beliefs. What beliefs about life, love, money, and health does your avatar behold? Do their beliefs help them live their perfect life? If yes - embrace them, and if no - choose to adopt and work on some new beliefs. Many think that there's nothing you can do about your beliefs. I disagree. Here are two approaches I use regularly to change my self-sabotaging beliefs into more self-supportive ones:

1. **I work with my hippocampus to create a more positive reel of my life.** Like neurolinguistic programming's timeline therapy, the hippocampal reset has helped me. I take time to visualize what can be possible for me. I imagined the tears running down my cheeks as I stood on the Olympic podium. Then, I zoomed in on the timeline and looked at other critical moments of my campaign on the way there. I saw our first competition, securing sponsorship and working with my veterinarians and farriers every four to six weeks. I saw the details of my journey and the end result. This visualization helped me set meaningful goals and choose my success habits to support them. Interestingly, I never had another show jumping pole down when I started using it! By the time Vesper got injured, I had learned so much more about the sport, the disciplines, and my power in the process! Don't let your fears keep you from shooting for the moon. Even if the unexpected happens and you don't make it, you may reach the stars on your way there.

2. **I release my negative cellular memory and replace it with positive experiences.** For example, I would challenge my old beliefs of stranger danger by showing myself evidence that not all people are predators. This approach convinces my Inner Children to let go of the black-and-white words like "always" and "never." It helps my cellular memory to not brace up against new people but to stay open and curious about them. With appropriate boundaries, I ask: "What don't I already know?".

Whether you use timelining through imagination or the release of cellular memory through action, remember that this process may take some time. Although challenging, letting go of who you used to be and making way for who you are becoming is one of the most empowering declarations of personal sovereignty.

You are so much more than the roles you have played throughout your life. You get to choose how you show up in the world and what duties you adopt along the way. Your unique intelligence is beautiful and powerful when you put it to work for you. Your values are important because they are important to *you*.

When you let go of aspects of you that no longer serve you, we all reap the benefits. Simply by interacting with you in the world, the rest of us can see glimmers of your genius as you dance toward your goals. While shame, guilt, and lack of confidence may trigger you to behave defensively at times, you can only deny your beauty for so long. When you rest in your genius more time than not, the light within you can illuminate the whole world.

You are you, a genius you. When you let your brilliance come alive through inspired action, we can all bask in the glory of your magnificence. Are you ready to harness your power?

Chapter 41

SIX STEPS TO HARNESSING YOUR POWER

*"Forget about the fast lane.
If you really want to fly,
just harness your power to your passion."*

- OPRAH WINFREY

Step 1: Claim your "me" time.

*H*ARNESSING YOUR POWER STARTS WITH **claiming the time** to do self-establishing exercises. You don't have to go sit on a mountaintop for thirty days to do this. It doesn't have to be a full day or even several hours. Some of the Sumiloff Academy students have claimed their "me" time in as little as ten minutes at a time.

However, I do recommend that you make "me" time a daily practice, and that you book it into your schedule. When you commit to prioritizing yourself daily, you create a new baseline of self-care. If you take time for yourself daily, you show yourself - through action - that you matter. By taking action, you challenge your cellular memory to relinquish any past ideas that you are unimportant.

The fact is that you **do** matter. Your life is **yours**. Claim it. Own it. Your needs matter, and your life matters. The world doesn't just need you to show up. The world needs you to show up as the full, unapologetic *you*. How can you be you if all you do is chase your tail or play roles that are inauthentic to you?

See your brilliance! If you can't see it yet, trust that it's there. I have yet to meet a non-pathological person who doesn't possess splendor and inner luminosity. No matter how busy you are, simply claiming ten minutes daily makes a statement to your subconscious mind - as well as everyone else - that you are the authority of your life.

Step 2: Discover what's important to you!

The second step to harnessing your power is to know **the values that make you feel alive**. Many argue that values are adopted from our parents or other people in perceived positions of power. As you know by now, our conditioning from others can influence our decision-making. But when it comes to our core values, they originate from the absence of something we needed when growing up.

Many, especially those of us who have experienced high levels of conditioning or abuse, can live shadow lives. These shadow lives are ones that we "should" live instead of ones that we want to live. In these cases, discovering your values can be challenging, but it's not impossible.

If you allow yourself to fail forward as you discover what's important to you, you can find out what makes you feel alive regardless of your past conditioning or pain. While this concept is simple, it's not necessarily easy. If you have experienced severe abuse and suppression, you may need the support of a certified 4 People Within® mentor or a mental health professional.

If you already know your life values, list them and build your days around them. It's easy to get swept up by the busyness of life and ignore what makes you feel alive. The distractions can zap your energy while living according to your values increases your levels of vitality. So, harness your inner power by failing forward as you attempt to live your "perfect day" every day.

Step 3: Hardwire yourself for success

Knowing and growing your cognitive capacity is the third step to harnessing your power. Your thoughts, emotions, intuition, and decided habits can be the best allies you have in this life. Why not harness their natural power?

According to the 4 People Within® model, you have a thinker, a feeler, an intuitive, and a sensor "person" within you. Two of them are your Inner Grown-ups, and two are your Inner Children. You can hardwire each of these parts for success. Suppose you know who your thinker is, who your feeler is, and who your intuitive and sensor are. In that case, you can discover your natural cognitive genius and be more joyous, compassionate, creative, and effective on your way to your "perfect day."

The job of the **thinker** is to shift through intentional thoughts, such as "What practices would make my life more aligned with my 'perfect day'?" and more detailed ones, such as "What time do I need to reserve for brain-storming my business today?". The thinker reasons, deducts, and counts pros and cons to help you make better decisions. Critical thinking is also deep within their wheelhouse. How do you see your thinker? Are you happy with how they are performing, or do you need to help that part of you grow and mature a bit more? Do you sometimes need more space to think before making an important decision?

The job of the **feeler** is to keep you connected with your passion and relationships. The feeler asks questions such as "What emotional encounters are necessary for me to live a 'perfect day'?" and, as a more precise example: "What action step do I need to take next to reactivate my passion project?" Are you happy with your feeler's performance, or would you like to see more passion and compassion in your life? Does your feeler need to mature to stay out of chaotic relationships going forward? What activity makes your heart sing, and are you prioritizing it?

The job of the **intuitive** within you is to develop new ideas and find meaning beyond the obvious. The intuitive asks questions like "What patterns and constructs are a part of my 'perfect day'?" and, more precisely, questions like "What meaning does this specific idea hold for me?". Are you feeling good about the number of meaningful ideas, patterns, and constructs you generate, or do you wish you were more imaginative, and able to easily shift perspective? Does the intuitive within you need like-minded support from others? Is the intuitive part of you being witnessed and embraced by you and those who love you?

The job of the **sensor** is to exist in the world, past and present. The sensor within us asks general questions like "What activities must happen in a day that is perfect for me?" and, more precisely, "What happened in the past with these activities, and what did I learn from what happened?" Do you have a sense of order in your current surroundings, or do you wish you had more power over the people, sounds, and smells around you? Are there specific activities or relationships that make you feel safe, and through what actions can you deepen those relationships?

Asking and answering these questions thoughtfully takes time. That's why step number one is claiming your "me" time. As long as we get to know and grow our cognitive capacity, we will continue to develop and strengthen our psyche and show up more authentically in life and our relationships.

How would it feel if you knew in your core that you'd be fine no matter what life throws at you? This is one of the greatest gifts that Inner Parenting yourself through the 4 People Within® protocol can give you. Having implemented this step, my life and its decisions have become more intentional and authentic. I no longer chase my tail throughout the day, only to feel depleted and directionless at the end of it. Once I engaged and deliberately attended to the needs of my inner thinker, feeler, intuitive, and sensor, I started to feel like *I* was in charge of my own life. I wish that same powerful feeling for you.

Step 4: Bridle your subconscious mind

Step four is **learning to direct your subconscious mind deliberately.** Some like to use the word "affirmations," but I call them captain's orders. Captain's orders are not some wishy-washy delusional statements we use to fool ourselves. We don't pretend that we can achieve something - such as becoming a billionaire - by simply wishing it was true.

Plenty of science and millions of personal examples speak to the power of harnessing your subconscious mind. Captain's orders are carefully chosen directions from our conscious mind to our subconscious mind about things we want to change in our lives. Our subconscious mind hears the orders and starts looking for ways to fulfill them. The conscious mind's intentional directions help your subconscious notice ideas, insights, and opportunities as they arise in your everyday life.

I remember utilizing this tool back in Dublin, Ireland. I was working in an auction house doing a job I was unhappy with. No matter what I did to change my attitude toward my job, it simply didn't work. I realized that the lesson this job would teach me was about demanding respect. I decided to redirect my brain from tolerating bad treatment to looking for a new job. I gave myself a conscious order, and my subconscious mind said, "Yes, ma'am." I was in a new job with the Olympic Council of Ireland within weeks. Despite some cultural hiccups, I thoroughly enjoyed working with the sports administration and the athletes. I stayed until the office moved to a location that was no longer accessible to me.

When it was time to pivot my career again, once more, I used the intentional direction of my subconscious mind. My captain's order for the new change was: "I want to learn how to have a part-time job close to home and start my massage business on the side." With the help of my dear friend Daf, I got an opportunity to do just that. She hired me part-time, and supported my bodywork business as well. I am forever grateful to her for that.

I recommend creating probable, realistic captain's orders. Something that stretches you a little but does not feel impossible. For example, instead of saying: "I'm getting my dream job tomorrow," you can say, "I'm open to finding my new dream job in the coming days/weeks."

If even that approach feels too much out of reach, begin using the word "learn." As in: "I am learning to open myself up for finding my new dream job in the coming days/weeks." This statement is true if you are willing to learn more about finding a dream job instead of being pressured to find one. Using the word "learn" can also be useful if you don't know what your dream job is! You can say: "I am learning more about what I want!" Some may think words are just semantics, but I don't agree. In my experience, they can be a powerful tool if put to work with intention and care.

Step 5: Lights, Camera, ...ACTION!

Next, to harness your power, you must **take action**. Knowing yourself is essential. Your intent is important. But without taking action in your life, your potential stays internal. Visualizing what you want without taking action around it is pure psychological entertainment, and I understand why most people get stuck at that level. It can be confronting to take action! Taking action means that you have to commit to your inner vision in the outside world.

You may be scared of being ridiculed and marginalized. It's true, that does happen - hell, as you know, it's happened to me. But I can't stress enough how much more pleasurable, connected, effective, and authentic your life becomes when you feel the fear and do it anyway.

You don't have to take massive action. In fact, small and consistent steps over time make your journey of realizing your vision more sustainable. By taking smaller steps and giving yourself time to orient yourself between the steps, you integrate the newest version of yourself as you go. By pacing yourself, harnessing your power becomes a steady practice on your way to your goal.

What is a small step you can take toward your vision today? What action aligns with your values and feels nurturing to each of your 4 People Within® (thinker, feeler, intuitive, and sensor)? It could be something as simple as committing to reading one book per month or booking time to sit by the river and observe the powerful flow of nature.

Step 6: Review and Revise

The final step of harnessing your power is to review and revise. At the end of each day, just before I go to bed, I take a moment and review the day. Here are the questions I ask myself before retiring for the night:

1. What went well?
2. What was a challenge that I learned from?
3. What else do I need to learn? Was there something that I hadn't figured out yet? (The next day, I set a captain's order around wanting to learn more about this).
4. What tension do I hold in my thoughts, feelings, or physical body? Could I release that pressure, even for a

moment? Would I be willing to release the stress, knowing that my subconscious mind will eventually resolve the issue? Am I prepared to release all tension right now?

5. What am I grateful for, and why?

Mastering this six-step routine of harnessing your power is not meant to be a quick fix. It may take years, but I invite you to compare that to how many years you've already invested in putting yourself down or not supporting yourself fully. How long have you already denied your pure brilliance? How long have you sabotaged your dreams by prioritizing those of others?

You matter. The legacy you leave behind matters. Is it time to invest in your most significant, incredible asset: **YOU**?

Remember that it will take some time to change the habits you have established in the past decades. If you have treated yourself poorly repeatedly, you may have convinced yourself that you are not worthy. But the good news is that flipping the narrative works, too. Getting to know yourself and deliberately embracing your natural strengths will condition you to discover a new level of self-respect and appreciation. When you start harnessing your power, living your "perfect day", and taking action on what is authentic to you, in time, your life - and your legacy - will reflect the incredible genius that is you. **Are you ready?**

Chapter 42

YOUR LEGACY

What you leave behind is not what is
engraved in stone monuments, but
what is woven into the lives of others.

- PERICLES

EVERY PERSON LEAVES A LEGACY of their spirit behind. How
you live and interact with others leaves a trail of your glow in the
world long after you are gone. As long as your spirit is alive in
others' hearts or their everyday lives, your legacy keeps living on.
So, what, my friend, is your legacy? Can we help you actualize it?

The glow I leave behind will be dark blue, pink, and gold. My
legacy is one of personal sovereignty, pure love, and freedom. My
fifty-year vision of creating a more joyous, compassionate, creative,
and effective world for us and future generations drives this legacy.
For my vision to actualize, I shall continue to share my reparenting
approach to help those who want to break free from their childhood
wounds and build a life that looks like them. I will continue to
support my students as they heal from their past trauma, develop
success skills, and confidently step into mastering their lives.

Will I always live perfectly according to my legacy? No, but I
won't stop doing my best, either. The journey doesn't have to be
perfect. I know that owning my imperfections and loving myself

despite of them can inspire others to forgive themselves for not being perfect. I hope that my love for my Inner Children continues to inspire others as they learn to love all parts of themselves without condition.

Regardless of the pain you have experienced, you are worthy! Mistakes are only mistakes if we refuse to learn from them. I hope my story of multiple "failures" but overall success has shown you how valuable we are despite our perceived flaws. I also hope this book has inspired you to be fully and wholly YOU, warts and all. I hope that this book has spurred you on to leave an intentional legacy of your unique glow behind.

Don't be afraid of the darkness! Remember that many of our greatest gifts to the world lie beneath our deepest wounds! No matter what adversity you have encountered, facing and befriending your pain can help you meet and befriend yourself more deeply. So, if it feels right for you, use your past pain as fuel for a better future. Don't be scared to make mistakes. Commit to yourself for better or for worse. The world needs you to be YOU!

Don't let the past generations decide your legacy. If you were left with a pile of manure, find the pony! This book and the Sumiloff online Academy are a healing manifestation of the vitriolic legacy my father left me. I took his energy and made it into something I believe his non-traumatized inner being would be proud of.

Having said that, I'm only getting started. The vision of the physical "safe houses" is being built through the Sumiloff Online Academy. If you are recovering from trauma and are used to being hyper-independent, know that the next step is to heal yourself in a safe community. We are here for you!

If you're ready for the next level of self-repair, join us at the Academy. Together, we can help our Inner Children heal and grow as we pursue a vision of a kinder, more whole world. We can all continue to share our "failures" as examples for each other. May we use them to teach one another how to love ourselves through challenging life experiences, and actualize our sovereign, free selves - starting exactly where we are! Don't let today's challenges define the rest of your life. Don't believe your most traumatized self when it tells you that you have no value. Don't let your most wounded self convince you that you're too broken to ever amount to anything.

The fact is that we continue to develop throughout our lives. Our thoughts and bodies will evolve as long as our brain has oxygen and can function. So, please remember one thing. Even if you're in deep despair, you're still breathing, and there is hope for a better tomorrow. You have already survived one hundred percent of your bad days. You can literally continue to build your legacy until your last day on this earth. **It's never too late.** Make every single day matter.

I rose from childhood sexual, psychological, alcoholic, and narcissistic abuse to this position of self-empowerment and global leadership. If I can heal, develop, and master my life, so can you! The genius within you is waiting to be discovered, recovered, and harnessed. Your legacy is being written **right now** as you read the final words of this book. So, my friend, don't be afraid to own your life: the good, the bad, and the beautiful.

You are beautiful.

The whole world benefits from your profound self-ownership, self-commitment, and self-knowledge.

Nothing is more glorious than the opportunity to bask in the radiance of your self-artistry.

Thank you for being who you are. Thank you for becoming all you are.

It has been an absolute privilege to share this journey with you.

Kindest regards,
Merja

GRATITUDE

Merja

Lisa - You have been a wonderful writing partner, confidant, and friend. You have kept me on the straight and narrow whenever I start veering off into the bushes. I appreciate you. Here's to many more!

Farita - Thank you for E-V-E-R-Y-T-H-I-N-G you have done for me.

Taheera, Virpi & Titta - I could not have done this without you.

My Inner Family - You are my everything.

My Family - I love you deeply.

To my Horses - You and I were meant to fly. Thank you.

Lisbeth - Thank you for being my best friend.

Céline Dion - You have been my constant companion. Thank you for sharing your genius with all of us.

Faieda - You are always in my heart.

Sabella, Alena & Zoe - Thank you for being in my life.

Alan & Robyn - thank you for being the best neighbors we could have hoped for.

Kevin L - the horses and I are grateful for you and your land.

The Robinsons - Your kindness and generosity has been life-giving.

Reino & family - Your generosity of spirit literally saved my life.

Niina - I believe everyone deserves a friend like you, especially when discovering who they are.

Sandy - You have kept me safe. I'm always in your debt.

Rani - Cheese, pretentious crackers, wine, and death. ;)

Victoria - Your support has meant the world to me. Thank you.

Louise - Thank you for your friendship.

Beck - Thank you for everything you are.

Soph - Here's to Paddock-Hippo, Dorito-ears, Ruby-the-lil'-red-horse & BV Murder Mystery. Big thanks to you and **Jono** for safe spaces for us and the horses.

Brian - Thank you for all the opportunities - and the food!

PJ - Thank you for your spirit, coffee, and hugs. You're a treasure!

Kiia - Thank you for being the perfect Canberra travel- and flatmate for an introverted writer.

Garry, Karina & Kurt - thank you for giving this introvert shelter to work through the final chapter.

Daf - I appreciate you greatly.

Dermot - You have lifted me up in some of my darkest moments. Thank you.

Ann, Kerry, Lynne & Pam - Thanks for taking me in when I most needed it.

Local friends and neighbors - I appreciate your connection and care.

Gosia (Sis), Monika & Wendy - Thank you for helping me get started.

Kikka - Thank you for taking me with you to the stables!

Thank you **Antonia** and **Joel** from **Personality Hacker** for believing in the value of my work back in the day.

A special thanks to **Dr. Ramani** for your groundbreaking work on narcissistic parental wounding. You have given my Inner Children a wholesome vocabulary they can use to feel heard. Your work has made my process of reparenting exponentially more effective.

A special thanks to **Somersby Animal Hospital** for their outstanding care, professionalism, and technical knowledge. You are the great people who keep our beloved furry friends healthy and safe. You - each veterinarian and veterinary technician - are irreplaceable.

All my Clients & Students: past, present, and future - Sharing this journey of joy, compassion, creativity, and effectiveness with you is profoundly meaningful. Thank you.

My mentors: James, Kevin, Linda, and Mike - Thank you for creating safe spaces for me.

My friends all around the world: You make my world go around!

For details of any resources mentioned in this book, please contact the Sumiloff Academy of Human Integration at desk@ merjasumiloff.com.

Lisa

Merja - Thank you so much for allowing me to write Safe Spaces with you. It has been an amazing learning experience, and I've enjoyed the entire process.

My Family and Friends - Thank you for being patient and supportive of my writing journey.

Christopher - Thank you for being proud of me.

Printed in the United States
by Baker & Taylor Publisher Services